THE CAUSES OF THE CIVIL WAR

THE CAUSES OF
THE CIVIL WAR

Institutional Failure or Human Blunder?

Edited by HANS L. TREFOUSSE
Brooklyn College, City University of New York

KRIEGER PUBLISHING COMPANY
MALABAR, FLORIDA

Cover illustration: Little Bo-Peep. *(The New York Public Library Print Division)*

Original Edition 1971
Reprint 1977
Reprint 1982 with corrections

Printed and Published by
ROBERT E. KRIEGER PUBLISHING CO., INC.
KRIEGER DRIVE,
MALABAR, FLORIDA 32950

Library of Congress Cataloging in Publication Data
Main entry under title:

The Causes of the Civil War.

  Bibliography: p.
  Contents: Slavery and race: Slavery, the sole cause/James Ford Rhodes. Slavery and the problem of race adjustment/Allan Nevins—Economic conflict: The approach of the second American revolution/Charles A. and Mary R. Beard. Commitment to laissez faire/William Appleman Williams—[etc.]
  1. United States—History—Civil War, 1861-1865— Causes—Addresses, essays, lectures. I. Trefousse, Hans Louis.
  E459.C36   973.7'11   81-23696
  ISBN 0-89874-472-5   AACR2

Printed in the United States of America

10   9   8   7   6   5

CONTENTS

The Ruins of the Northwest Depot, Charleston, South Carolina, 1865. (*The National Archives*)

INTRODUCTION

The Civil War has always held a particular fascination for Americans. Its impact on the United States was so immense and its results so far-reaching that every generation since 1861 has sought to reinterpret it. What were the causes that led to the catastrophe? Why did the American system break down in the 1850s and 1860s? Who was responsible for the war, and how could the holocaust have been prevented? These are the questions that have been posed over and over again, until a vast literature on the war has accumulated.

Since the causation of wars is one of the central questions of history, it is not surprising that this, the most destructive conflict between 1815 and 1914, has received a great deal of attention. And indeed, for the study of the origins of human conflict, the American Civil War offers a rich field for research. Fought between two antagonists equally schooled in parliamentary methods, in a society where newspapers and periodicals sought to record all major events in as much detail as possible, it has been studied so minutely that virtually every step of the major participants, every action of any consequence, has been the subject of historical inquiry. The manuscript depositories of the country have been scoured for the most minute scraps of evidence bearing on the conflict; national Civil War Round Tables have been established, and several publications have devoted themselves almost exclusively to it. But in spite of all the study which has already taken place, there is no sign of a lessening of interest. Books continue to pour from the presses, doctoral candidates write their dissertations, and college courses are structured around the Civil War and Reconstruction. The war goes on.

The basic outlines of events are clear enough. The existence of slavery in the South, the rise of abolitionism in the North, the persistence of an agrarian society at odds with a growing industrialism, differences in constitutional interpretation, and the failure of the democratic process to resolve these problems, all contributed to an explosive situation in which war between the sections might break out at any moment. The crisis came in 1860–61, when, after the split in the Democratic party on the question of the desirability of a federal slave code for the territories, the Republicans won the presidential election on a platform of nonextension of the "peculiar institution," and the cotton states seceded. President Abraham Lincoln then attempted to send food to beleaguered Fort Sumter, the isolated federal post in Charleston harbor, and the government of the newly formed Southern Confederacy decided to reduce the fort by force. Civil war was the result. Although all these occurrences have been extensively described, the emphasis given to the various factors contributing to the debacle has differed widely.

In view of the far-reaching coverage of the conflict and of the length of time that has elapsed since the appearance of the first books dealing with the war, it is astonishing how frequently the same explanations have recurred. That slavery was a major factor in bringing on the war was clear to contemporaries, many of whom tended to take an extremely simplistic view of the national tragedy. Henry Wilson, radical Republican and later Vice President of the United States, was certain that the slaveholders had caused the war, which he explained in terms of the *History of the Rise and Fall of the Slave Power in America*, as he entitled his three-volume work published during the Reconstruction period. Economic factors, likewise, have been stressed from the very beginning. As early as 1884, James G. Blaine, in his *Twenty Years of Congress*, emphasized the importance of the economic conflict between the agrarian South and the industrial North, and in 1861, before the war had even started, Robert Toombs, in his secession speech in the Senate, pointed to alleged Northern intentions of outlawing $4,000,000,000 worth of property as a cause for war. The constitutional issue of states rights versus nationalism was the theme of the postwar reflections of Alexander H. Stephens, the former Vice President of the Confederacy. *A Constitutional View of the Late War Between the States*, he called his book, and his old opponent, Jefferson Davis, adopted a very similar point of view. Any number of writers sought to find the explanation in the actions of extremists. Northerners like General John A. Logan, who entitled his book *The Great Conspiracy*, held the fire-eaters responsible, and Southern sympathizers like Rushmore G. Horton, the abolitionists.

As time went on, the arguments became more sophisticated, but their fundamental tenor did not change materially. By the turn of the century, a nationalist school had developed, largely centered in the North and represented by scholars like James F. Rhodes, Hermann E. von Holst, and John Burgess. These writers tended to view the national state as a supreme good and condemned the South's particularistic attitudes, although they often sympathized with the minority section's racist outlook. By the 1920s, when Edward Channing titled the sixth volume of his *History of the United States, The War for Southern Independence*, the concept of two rival civilizations had arisen, an explanation which in part had been offered by Edward Pollard as early as 1866, and by the 1930s, the economic interpretation had been restated most effectively by Charles A. and Mary R. Beard. Then, shortly before the outbreak of the Second World War, the so-called revisionist school, consisting of historians like James G. Randall and Avery O. Craven, reverted to the anti-extremist point of view, spoke of a "repressible conflict," a needless war that might have been prevented, and stressed the breakdown of the American political system.

In view of the importance of ideological and racial factors since 1945, slavery and the conflict to which it gave rise have once more attracted attention. Not that these aspects had ever been wholly neglected. Critics of abolitionism like Frank L. Owsley and Gilbert H. Barnes had earlier published works dealing with them. But writers like Arthur Schlesinger, Jr. succeeded in restating in forceful terms the moral issue confronting the nation, and the concomitant problem of racial adjustment has been more extensively studied than before. Although John S. Rosenberg, questioning the values of Northern society, has doubted whether the war justified its cost, and Arnold Whitridge has once again attacked the extremists, writers like Richard H. Sewall and Hans L. Trefousse have defended the Northern radicals, and David M. Potter, in a major synthesis of the pre-war decade, has once more emphasized the centrality of slavery in causing the sectional conflict.

The other theories of the causation of the war have also received renewed attention. A modern formulation of the economic thesis has been written by Barrington Moore, who has characterized the conflict as a last offensive of middle class democracy. William Appleman Williams, a firm believer in the expansionist nature of laissez-faire society, has likewise explained the war in economic terms, as has Raimondo Luraghi, who has stressed the resistance of the South to industrial "modernization." Eugene D. Genovese, delineating the total domination of society by the Southern ruling class, has restated the class conflict in a new form. In support of the "two civilizations" school, Eric Foner has stressed the devotion of Northern Republicans to a society of free enterprise. The difficulties of maintaining the cohesion of the Democratic party have been analyzed by Roy F. Nichols, those of a party system devoid of issues by Michael F. Holt, constitutional controversies by Arthur Bestor, institutional shortcomings by David Donald, Southern expansionism by William Barney, and the defense of narrowly conceived Southern honor by Don E. Fehrenbacher. But however the emphasis may have changed, the basic causes of slavery, economic conflict, constitutional strife, political breakdown, and supposed extremist intransigence have recurred again and again. It seems that no serious student of the war can conscientiously ignore these factors.

What is true of the fundamental causes of the war is equally true of the immediate origins of the conflict. So tangled is the web of evidence bearing on the firing on Fort Sumter that ever since General Pierre G. T. Beauregard gave orders for the first shot all manner of explanations have been offered. Southern apologists from the very beginning have blamed the Union government in general and President Lincoln in particular for forcing the issue, while Northerners with equal plausibility have argued that the guilt is clear: Jefferson Davis and the government at Montgomery ordered the fort to be reduced by force, authorized the first shot, and therefore must bear full responsibility for the bloodshed that ensued. Modern historians have further divided upon the issue of Lincoln's motives: Did the President, in ordering the expedition for the relief of Fort Sumter, desire to provoke war in such a way as to throw guilt upon the South; did he wish to prevent war by sending only supplies and giving due notice to the Governor of South Carolina; or did he consciously take a risk of provoking war without necessarily desiring it? Since the evidence bearing upon this question is incomplete, it is likely that the controversy will continue unabated.

The selections which follow are excerpts representative of the major schools of thought on the causes of the Civil War. The first section deals with those historians who have emphasized either slavery or the racial issue. James Ford Rhodes, the author of the monumental work, *History of the United States from the Compromise of 1850,* wrote at a time when the immediate passions of the post-war era had cooled, but when it was still possible to assert, as he did, that "slavery was the sole cause of the war." Living in a period in which racism was on the increase, his attitude toward the blacks was at best ambivalent, but the power of his prose and the meticulous care with which he examined his sources have made his work a classic. Believing that the system of chattel slavery was outmoded and a blot on civilization, he concludes that the great failure of the South had been its inability to solve the question long before the Civil War. That the defense of human bondage was joined with the idea of state sovereignty is to him a fatal step in the development of a sectional spirit which finally drove an entire population into an unrighteous war for the protection of slavery. But he does not roundly condemn the slaveholders. Considering the "peculiar institution" a curse for North and South alike, he merely sees them as victims of their social system.

Allan Nevins, writing after World War II, when the emphasis on slavery as an explanation for the outbreak of the conflict was once more becoming popular, set out to cover again the ground previously gone over by Rhodes. In a series of volumes entitled, *Ordeal of the Union, The Emergence of Lincoln,* and *The War for the Union,* Nevins did not merely reexamine Rhodes' premises but added his insights as one of the most productive scholars in America, a historian who consulted virtually every available manuscript collection bearing on the period. His conclusions were similar to Rhodes'. Like his predecessor, he finds the Southern system wanting, and severely criticizes Stephen A. Douglas for introducing the Kansas-Nebraska Act, which repealed the Missouri Compromise and set in train a series of events leading directly to the Civil War. But, mindful of the overriding issues of his own day, Nevins stresses the racial problem with greater understanding. It is one of his major contentions that slavery was not merely a system of human bondage but also one of racial exploitation, and his explanations for the conflict are no longer so simplistic as Rhodes'. While giving due emphasis to constitutional, political, and economic factors, Nevins nevertheless once again emphasizes slavery and "its concomitant of racial adjustment" as the main problem leading to war. His provocative analysis has stimulated much further research, and in a recent reconsideration in "The Irrepressible Conflict," a chapter in his *The Imperiled Union,* Kenneth M. Stampp has reached similar conclusions.

But was slavery the chief cause of the war? Scholars who believe in the economic interpretation of the origins of the conflict have offered differing interpretations, here represented by two selections. One is an excerpt from Charles A. and Mary R. Beard's *The Rise of American Civilization,* and the other, part of a chapter of William Appleman Williams' *The Contours of American History.* A longtime member of the faculty of Columbia University, Charles A. Beard first became famous in 1913 with the publication of *An Economic Interpretation of the Constitution of the United States.* A series of important studies followed, and he became the best-known representative of a school which believed economic rivalries to hold the key to great historical events. Because of this outlook, Beard and his followers tended to play down the importance of ideological factors such as the crusade against slavery. To them the conflict between the agrarians of the South and the industrialists of the North—a version of the class struggle—seemed sufficient explanation of the origins of America's greatest holocaust. That this interpretation enjoyed great popularity during the economic depression of the 1930s, and that Marxists adopted it with some modifications, is not surprising.

How valid were the Beards' assumptions? Were Northern capitalists really united in outlook and goals? Did the owners of large Southern plantations invariably occupy positions in the forefront of the secession movement? Modern writers have questioned both concepts. But the economic interpretation has not been abandoned. An example of a more recent approach is represented by William Appleman Williams, primarily a specialist in the history of American foreign policy, whose views have been strongly influenced by Marxist positions. Williams believes both North and South to have been expansionist. The South, according to this view, wanted to expand its plantation system toward the Caribbean. The North, on the other hand, was committed to a laissez-faire society. And laissez faire, in Williams' opinion, invariably involved westward and overseas expansion. Consequently, he argues that the demand for a society in which laissez-faire attitudes could have free rein led both Northern businessmen and Western agrarians to combine against Southern slaveholders. The antislavery movement, he holds, was chiefly motivated by economic considerations, and he looks upon Stephen A. Douglas, William H. Seward, and Abraham Lincoln as advance agents of the "*Weltanschauung* of laissez faire." This attitude, he concludes, made impossible the peaceful settlement of the differences between the sections. Although Williams' sweeping generalizations have not been widely accepted, they are a good example of the more recent contributions of economic determinists.

Can one single factor alone explain historical events? Much more comprehensive than the economic interpretation of the causes of the Civil War is the "two civilizations" school. The selections included consist of excerpts from Arthur C. Cole's *The Irrepressible Conflict* and Frank L. Owsley's essay by the same title in the compendium written by twelve Southerners, *I'll Take My Stand.* One of the volumes in the *History of American Life* series which emphasized social and economic developments rather than politics, Professor Cole's work clearly illustrates the increasingly thorough division between the sections in all lines of endeavor. This differentiation, accentuated by the emergence of industry in the North and the persistence of slavery in the South, made it increasingly difficult for the plantation system to survive. While Cole does not specifically make the point, it is evident that he believes war to have been the result, and, like Rhodes and Nevins, he broadly sympathizes with the North and its opposition to the outmoded and cruel institution of human bondage.

Not so Frank L. Owsley. Southern-born and Southern-educated, Owsley does not hesitate to defend his section and the type of civilization which it cherished. To him, the main difference between North and South was not the institution of slavery, but the persistence of an agrarian society with its concomitant of slavery in one section and its disappearance in the other. His essay ably puts forth a view no longer popular, and it serves as an important counterweight to Cole's analysis.

The next group of selections deals with the failure of the political system as one of the main causes of the Civil War. James G. Randall's presidential address before the Mississippi Valley Historical Association at Omaha on May 2, 1940, "A Blundering Generation," most clearly illustrates this point of view. "If one word or phrase were selected to account for the war, that word would not be slavery, or state rights," he asserted. "It would have to be such a word as fanaticism (on both sides), or misunderstanding, or perhaps politics." As he sees it, men made the war; they might just as easily have prevented it.

Like Randall, Roy F. Nichols examines the problem of the breakdown of the American political process. After many years of research in the history of the Democratic party in the 1850s, he published in 1948 *The Disruption of American Democracy,* a book in which he summed up his conclusions. In this penetrating analysis, he emphasizes the importance of the party structure in holding American society together. As long as the united Democratic party was in existence, it could cope with the sectional, emotional, and ideological conflicts threatening the Union; once it broke apart, the last bulwark against disaster had been removed. Like Randall, he stresses the shortcomings of the political process, but in many ways, he is more interested in institutional defects than in individual failure.

To what degree moral indignation contributed to the outbreak of the war has long been a subject of controversy among historians. It was part of Randall's argument that extremists on both sides, both abolitionists and fire-eaters, were responsible, and Avery O. Craven, like Randall a representative of the revisionist school of the 1930s and 1940s, was generally critical of Northern radicals and abolitionists. But did not the continued existence of slavery involve a real moral issue? Could a Western democratic country permit so anachronistic an institution to go unchallenged? The next selection, excerpts from Arthur M. Schlesinger,

Jr.'s article in the *Partisan Review* for 1949, "The Causes of the Civil War: A Note on Historical Sentimentalism," addresses itself to this question. Severely criticizing the revisionists' failure to condemn slavery, Schlesinger rejects "sentimental theories about the needlessness of the Civil War." "We cannot be relieved from the duty of moral judgment on issues so appalling and inescapable as those involving human slavery," he writes, thus restating the convictions of many of his predecessors in modern terms.

Once the fundamental causes of the Civil War have been determined, the subsidiary question of the immediate background of the conflict, especially the firing of the first shot at Fort Sumter, still remains. The last portion of the book deals with this problem. Did Lincoln desire peace or did he seek to break the impasse by challenging the Confederate authorities to make an aggressive move? Or did he engage in a deliberate gamble? The first selection, Charles W. Ramsdell's article, "Lincoln and Fort Sumter," reprinted from the *Journal of Southern History*, represents the extreme pro-Southern viewpoint. Arguing that Lincoln, because of his difficulties, had decided that there was no other way than war "for the salvation of his administration, his party, and the Union," Ramsdell holds the President responsible for the consequences. According to this view, Lincoln arranged things in such a way as to maneuver "the Confederates into firing the first shot in order that they, rather than he, should take the blame of beginning the bloodshed." But does the evidence bear out such an interpretation? Neither James G. Randall nor David M. Potter were convinced by Ramsdell's arguments. Both held that Lincoln was interested in preserving peace, and that all his actions pointed to this desire. The selection included is the Preface to the 1962 edition of Potter's book, *Lincoln and His Party in the Secession Crisis*. When in 1942 he had first published his findings, Potter had written that Lincoln's policy "offered maximum possibilities of avoiding conflict; a Confederate attack to prevent food from going to Sumter would constitute an offensive act; therefore Lincoln, wishing to save Sumter without a fight, sought to hold it by a policy so purely defensive that the South would hesitate to make an issue of it." Twenty years later, with additional evidence available because of the opening in 1947 of the Robert Todd Lincoln Papers, the author saw no reason to revise his opinions.

How valid were Potter's and Randall's conclusions? Reexamining the evidence, Richard N. Current, excerpts from whose book, *Lincoln and the First Shot*, constitute the final selection, arrives at slightly different conclusions. After carefully reviewing the evidence concerning the events leading to the attack on the fort and the historical controversies to which they have given rise, he argues that Lincoln, in ordering the relief expedition, was taking a calculated risk. In this assessment, he is in substantial agreement with Kenneth P. Stampp, whose study, *And the War Came*, also dealt with the immediate background of the war.

Thus, after over one hundred years of intense study, both the underlying and immediate causes of the Civil War are still in dispute, and it becomes questionable whether the issue will ever be fully resolved. Undoubtedly, every generation will continue to interpret it according to its own predilections. It is to be hoped that the continuing controversy will shed additional light, not merely on the American Civil War, but also on the fundamental causes of human conflict in general. The time and energy expended on it will then have been worthwhile.

JAMES FORD RHODES (1848–1927) turned to the
writing of history in 1885 after a successful career in
business. His *History of the United States from the
Compromise of 1850*, a tribute to his scholarship as well
as his industry, is marked by an absence of wartime
passions, although it is broadly nationalistic in outlook.
The selection which follows is indicative of his
insistence that slavery was the sole cause of the Civil
War.*

James Ford Rhodes

Slavery, the Sole Cause

In the election of Lincoln the North had spoken. Because slavery was wrong, the majority of the Northern people had declared against its extension. South Carolina quickly made answer. Before the October elections, men in that State believed the choice of Lincoln probable, and after Pennsylvania and Indiana had gone Republican, only a lingering hope remained that the issue could be other than that dreaded by the South. The minds of men were preparing for action in case the event should actually take place. It was argued that honor and pecuniary interest alike demanded disunion. There seemed little doubt that public opinion would support the political leaders of the State in promptly taking measures to put in force the long-threatened remedy of secession. Gist, South Carolina's governor, shaped with alacrity his official action in conformity to the sentiment of his State. Before the October elections he had sent a confidential letter to each of the governors of the cotton States, with the exception of Houston of Texas, saying that South Carolina would unquestionably consider her course in convention and asking for cooperation on the part of her sister States. October 12, three days after Pennsylvania and Indiana had virtually decided the presidential contest, Gist called the usual session of the legislature for the purpose of appointing presidential electors; but at the same time he gave the unusual intimation that some action

*James Ford Rhodes, *History of the United States from the Compromise of 1850*, Vol. III (New York: The Macmillan Co., 1895), pp. 114–125, 146–149, 272–280, 324–325. (Footnotes omitted).

might be necessary "for the safety and protection of the State." November 5, the day before the election, the legislature assembled at Columbia. Governor Gist recommended that in case Lincoln was elected provision should be made immediately for the holding of a convention in the view of severing the connection of South Carolina with the Federal Union. . . .

If any one is inclined to doubt that there was other than a single cause for secession and the war that ensued; if he feel himself almost persuaded by the earnest and pathetic statements of Southern writers since the war, who naturally have sought to place the four years' devotion and heroism of the South on a higher basis than that of a mighty effort to conserve an institution condemned alike by Christianity and by ethics, let him read the speeches and the newspaper articles of the early days of the secession movement in South Carolina. It cannot be denied that the South Carolinians looked the matter squarely in the face, and that sincerity characterized their utterances. "The first issue," said Trenholm, "was made upon the question of a tariff in which the sympathies of the world were with the South. Now we are joining the issue with the prejudices and the sympathies of the world against us." "The question is," declared a preacher in a Sunday sermon, whether slavery "is an institution to be cherished," or whether it "must be dispensed with." While South Carolinians did not for a moment doubt the right of secession, they were not ignorant of the fact that their movement might be called revolution. "It is not a legislative revolution, but a popular revolution," truly said a member of the legislature at the Thursday meeting, and a similar manner of expression is common in the political literature of the time. . . .

Charleston and South Carolina people

felt that secession was no longer a choice, but a necessity; that they had submitted to as much aggression from the North as a free people could endure and preserve their liberties. It is a striking evidence of the mutual misunderstanding between the two sections that, while eleven twelfths of the Northern voters thought the South had lorded it over the North since the annexation of Texas, South Carolinians, almost to a man, and the majority of the men of the cotton States, were equally convinced that they had suffered grievous wrongs from the North. This sentiment was now strong in South Carolina. When her people acknowledged the greater prosperity of the North, they asserted that it had been obtained at the expense of the South by protective tariffs. In the event of separation, the South Carolinians had dreams of unrestricted direct trade with Europe, which would redound to the advantage of their agricultural interests, and would make Charleston rival Boston and New York in commercial importance. They considered the admission of California in 1850 as a free State an outrage, and asserted that insult was added to injury in the resistance by State legislation and by mobs to the enforcement of the Fugitive Slave law, when that law had been conceded by the North as an offset for the gain which destroyed the equilibrium between the two sections. The urging of the commercial question, the assertion that the South suffered grievously from the tariff acts, was a survival from 1832, and was one of those lesser arguments that are popularly supposed to add somewhat of strength to the main cause; but it did not touch the vital matter. The grievance regarding slavery resolved itself into a fierce resistance to the virtual reproach of the Republican party that the South Carolinians were living in the daily practice of a heinous wrong.

If the negro had never been brought to

America and enslaved, South Carolina would not have seceded. Nothing in all history is plainer than that the ferment of which I have been speaking was due solely to the existence of slavery. That the North had been encroaching upon the South, that it had offered an indignity in the election of Lincoln, was for South Carolinians a feeling perfectly natural, and it was absolutely sincere. The President-elect believed that slavery should ultimately be done away with, while they were convinced that it was either a blessing, or else the only fit and possible condition of the negro in contact with the white. That their cause was the cause of life, liberty, and property seemed, from their point of view, beyond question. No South Carolinian would have maintained that any overt act of oppression had yet been committed, but he would have asserted that a free people must strike at the first motion of tyranny, while for an example he might have pointed to the sons of Massachusetts in the years that preceded the American Revolution. It soon began to be apparent that the course on which the State was entering involved sacrifice as well as excited enthusiasm. Business grew bad, merchants found it difficult and even impossible to pay their debts, and, before the end of November, the banks of Charleston were forced to suspend specie payments. But the people showed no signs of faltering. During the month of November there were a round of meetings, pole-raisings, dedications of banners, fireworks, and illuminations; and the music of this nascent revolution was the Marseillaise.

Interest now became centred on the next formal step to be taken in the march of secession. December 6 had been fixed as the day on which delegates to the convention should be chosen. Voters did not divide on party lines. Indeed, since 1851, political divisions, such as were seen in the other Southern States, did not exist in South Carolina. Had the popular vote for President obtained there as elsewhere, the voice for Breckinridge would undoubtedly have been almost unanimous. The lines of 1851, of separate State action or cooperation, were sometimes referred to, but they were obliterated by the actual unanimity of sentiment. Had there been a union party or a party of delay, a contest would have been natural, but no such parties existed. It was a favorite notion of some Northern observers that a latent union sentiment existed in South Carolina, but that it was kept under by intimidation. Anonymous letters may be found scattered through the Northern journals of this period, which, were they representative, would go to substantiate this belief. But all other contemporary evidence points to the view that I have taken. It is almost certain that the nonslaveholding whites were as eager for secession as the slave-owners. The antipathy of race, always strong, had been powerfully excited by assertions that submission meant the freeing of the negroes and the bestowal on them of civil rights, and by the statement, often repeated and currently believed, that Vice-President-elect Hamlin was a mulatto.

The fact that the South, in its sentiment on slavery, was at war with the rest of the civilized world, undoubtedly lent arrogance to assertions of South Carolinians and intolerance to their acts. They were especially severe on Northerners suspected in any way of propagating abolition opinions. An example of this is seen in the action of the book-shops of Charleston, in closing their accounts with the publishers of *Harper's Weekly* and *Magazine,* and returning all the copies on hand, because the *Weekly* had published a biographical sketch and full-length portrait of Abraham Lincoln. Yet the experience of Petigru would seem to show that a union party headed by South Carolinians of character and position would have obtained a hearing and been permitted to advocate unmolested their views. The election of delegates to the convention did not turn on any party differences, nor were the candidates nominated by parties. In some places they were put up by public meetings; in Charleston the nominations were made through the advertising columns of the newspapers. The election turned on the personal standing and ability of the candidates, and, in the main, the most distinguished men of the State were chosen. Of the twenty-two delegates elected from the Charleston district, seventeen had declared for prompt secession and forever against reunion, three favored secession as soon as practicable, and two did not respond to the inquiries of the Charleston *Mercury;* but one of these was C. G. Memminger, afterwards Secretary of the Treasury of the Southern Confederacy, and he had declared in a speech that "secession is a necessity, not a choice."

Thus stood affairs on December 3, when Congress met. South Carolina was practically unanimous for secession; the President had failed utterly to rise to the emergency, while at the North there existed an overwhelming desire to preserve the Union. All eyes were directed towards Congress. Would it avert the threatened danger? As the persistent attitude of South Carolina and the warm sympathy with her of her sister States were fixed facts, the question was, What would the Republicans in Congress be willing to do to satisfy the South? Compromise had solved the difficulty in 1820, in 1833, and in 1850; and it was now apparent that the border State men and the Northern Democrats could unite on a plan which would prevent the secession of all the States except South Carolina. Would the

Republicans go as far as that? Properly to judge their action in this crisis, we must first inquire, what were the grievances of the South as made known to Congress?

The tangible grievances were the interference with the execution of the Fugitive Slave act by the Personal Liberty laws, and the denial by the North to the owners of negro slaves of the common rights of property in the territories. The wrong done the South by the Personal Liberty laws was dwelt upon by men who were opposed to secession, and who, taking an impregnable position, were willing to rest their case upon a remediable complaint. Their conspicuous exponent was Alexander H. Stephens. In the famous speech which he made before the Georgia legislature, November 14, he thrust this view into prominence. His words gave rise to much discussion. It may be positively affirmed that, if the sole grievance of the South had been the alleged nullification of the Fugitive Slave act by many Northern States, there would have been no secession but that of South Carolina. For this grievance would certainly have been redressed. Vermont, the pioneer in this sort of legislation, had already taken steps towards the revision of her Personal Liberty act. On December 17 the national House of Representatives, in which the Republicans and anti-Lecompton Democrats had a clear majority, earnestly recommended, by a vote of 153 to 14, the repeal of the Personal Liberty laws in conflict with the Constitution. These facts, with others that will be mentioned later, show that, if it would have appeased the South, every State, with the possible exception of Massachusetts, either would have rescinded this legislation, or so modified it that it no longer would have been an offence. Early in the session of Congress, however, the Republicans were told that this would not settle the difficulty. "You talk about repealing the Personal Liberty bills as a concession to the South," said Senator Iverson of Georgia. "Repeal them all tomorrow, sir, and it would not stop the progress of this revolution." Iverson spoke for a large party in the empire State of the South. Since the secession of South Carolina had become a foregone conclusion, the action of Georgia was awaited with breathless interest, and every indication of her sentiment was scanned with care. "What though all the Personal Liberty bills were repealed," asked Jefferson Davis, the leader of the cotton States; "would that secure our rights?"

The other tangible grievance—the refusal of the North to recognize that the slaveholder's human chattels had the common attributes of other property in the territories—was urged with emphasis by Davis and by Toombs. It was indeed replied that the Dred Scott decision gave them all that they claimed, but to this it was naturally rejoined that the President-elect did not accept as binding the general principle in regard to slave property as asserted by Chief-Justice Taney. The experience of the last seven years had made patent to each party the importance of a friendly executive, when the issue of freedom and slavery should come to be fought out in the territories.

 The intangible grievance of the South was the sentiment of the North in regard to slavery. In most of the public declarations and confidential letters one is struck with the influence with the stigma cast by Republicans upon the slaveholders had on the Southern mind. This sensitiveness proved to be a heavy obstacle in the way of compromise. Between the idea that slavery was right, or, at least, the only suitable condition of the negro, and the idea that slavery was a blot upon the nation, it seemed wellnigh impossible to hit upon the common ground of opinion which was a necessary antecedent to compromise. "The true cause of our danger," declared Jefferson Davis, "I believe to be that a sectional hostility has been substituted for a general fraternity. . . . Where is the remedy?" he asked. "In the hearts of the people" is the ready reply.

If, after the evidence I have already adduced, any one doubts that slavery was the sole cause of the war, and that, had it not existed, the doctrine of States-rights would never have been pushed to the extreme remedy of secession, let him consider the proceedings of these conventions, and give especial attention to the justifications of Mississippi and Georgia. The convention of Mississippi declared that "Our position is thoroughly identified with the institution of slavery. . . . A blow at slavery is a blow at commerce and civilization. . . . There was no choice left us but submission to the mandates of abolition, or a dissolution of the Union." Toombs's report, adopted by the Georgia convention, was of the same tenor. . . .

When one thinks of the many fruitless attempts of peoples to devise wise systems of government, and of the many admirable constitutions on paper which have been adopted, but which have failed to find a response in the character and political habits of the men for whom they were intended, one might be lost in admiration at the orderly manner in which the Southerners proceeded, at the excellent organic instrument they adopted, at the ready acceptance of the work of their representatives, were it not that they were running amuck against the civilized world in their attempt to bolster up human slavery, and in their theory of governmental particularism, when the spirit of the age was tending to freedom and to unity. The sincerest and frankest public man in the

Southern Confederacy, Alexander H. Stephens, told the true story. "The new constitution has put at rest forever," he declared, "all the agitating questions relating to our peculiar institution— African slavery as it exists amongst us— the proper status of the negro in our form of civilization. This was the immediate cause of the late rupture and present revolution. . . . The prevailing ideas entertained by Jefferson and most of the leading statesmen at the time of the formation of the old Constitution were, that the enslavement of the African was in violation of the laws of nature, that it was wrong in principle socially, morally, and politically. . . .

"Our new government is founded upon exactly the opposite idea; its foundations are laid, its corner-stone rests, upon the great truth that the negro is not equal to the white man; that slavery—subordination to the superior race—is his natural and normal condition. This, our new government, is the first in the history of the world based upon this great physical, philosophical, and moral truth. . . .

"The great objects of humanity are best attained when there is conformity to the Creator's laws and decrees, in the formation of governments as well as in all things else. Our confederacy is founded upon principles in strict conformity with these laws. This stone, which was rejected by the first builders, 'is become the chief of the corner'—the real 'corner-stone'—in our new edifice."

ALLAN NEVINS (1890–   ) is one of the most prolific
of modern American historians. Already distinguished
as the author of significant works in virtually all phases
of the development of the United States, after the
Second World War he published the first volumes of a
projected overall history of the country since 1847.
Although in the following excerpts from *The
Emergence of Lincoln* he, too, emphasizes the
importance of slavery as a cause of the war, his analysis
is somewhat different from Rhodes'. What are the chief
points of divergence between the two authors?*

Allan Nevins

Slavery and the Problem of
Race Adjustment

Great and complex events have great
and complex causes. Burke, in his *Reflections on the Revolution in France,* wrote
that "a state without the means of some
change is without the means of its conservation," and that a constant reconciliation
of "the two principles of conservation and
correction" is indispensable to healthy
national growth. It is safe to say that every
such revolutionary era as that on which
the United States entered in 1860 finds
its genesis in an inadequate adjustment of
these two forces. It is also safe to say that
when a tragic national failure occurs, it
is largely a failure of leadership. "Brains
are of three orders," wrote Machiavelli,
"those that understand of themselves,
those that understand when another

shows them, and those that understand
neither by themselves nor by the showing
of others." Ferment and change must
steadily be controlled; the real must, as
Bryce said, be kept resting on the ideal;
and if disaster is to be avoided, wise leaders must help thoughtless men to understand, and direct the action of invincibly
ignorant men. Necessary reforms may be
obstructed in various ways; by sheer in-
ertia, by tyranny and class selfishness, or
by the application of compromise to basic
principles—this last being in Lowell's
view the main cause of the Civil War.
Ordinarily the obstruction arises from a
combination of all these elements. To
explain the failure of American leadership in 1846–1861, and the revolution that

*Reprinted with the permission of Charles Scribner's Sons from Volume II, *The Emergence of Lincoln,*
pp. 462–471, by Allan Nevins. Copyright 1950 Charles Scribner's Sons.

ensued, is a bafflingly complicated problem.

Looking backward from the verge of war in March, 1861, Americans could survey a series of ill-fated decisions by their chosen agents. One unfortunate decision was embodied in Douglas's Kansas-Nebraska Act of 1854. Had an overwhelming majority of Americans been ready to accept the squatter sovereignty principle, this law might have proved a statesmanlike stroke; but it was so certain that powerful elements North and South would resist it to the last that it accentuated the strife and confusion. Another disastrous decision was made by Taney and his associates in the Dred Scott pronouncement of 1857. Still another was made by Buchanan when he weakly accepted the Lecompton Constitution and tried to force that fraudulent document through Congress. The Northern legislatures which passed Personal Liberty Acts made an unhappy decision. Most irresponsible, wanton, and disastrous of all was the decision of those Southern leaders who in 1858–60 turned to the provocative demand for Congressional protection of slavery in all the Territories of the republic.* Still other errors might be named. Obviously, however, it is the forces behind these decisions which demand our study; the waters pouring down the gorge, not the rocks which threw their spray into the air.

At this point we meet a confused clamor of voices as various students attempt an explanation of the tragic denouncement of 1861. Some writers are as content with a

simple explanation as Lord Clarendon was when he attributed the English Civil War to the desire of Parliament for an egregious domination of the government. The bloody conflict, declared James Ford Rhodes, had "a single cause, slavery." He was but echoing what Henry Wilson and other early historians had written, that the aggressions of the Slave Power offered the central explanation. That opinion had been challenged as early as 1861 by the London *Saturday Review,* which remarked that "slavery is but a surface question in American politics," and by such Southern propagandists as Yancey, who tried to popularize a commercial theory of the war, emphasizing a supposed Southern revolt against the tariff and other Yankee exactions. A later school of writers was to find the key to the tragedy in an inexorable conflict between the business-minded North and the agrarian-minded South, a thrusting industrialism colliding with a rather static agricultural society. Still another group of writers has accepted the theory that the war resulted from psychological causes. They declare that agitators, propagandists, and alarmists on both sides, exaggerating the real differences of interest, created a state of mind, a hysterical excitement, which made armed conflict inevitable.

At the very outset of the war Senator Mason of Virginia, writing to his daughter, asserted that two systems of society were in conflict; systems, he implied, as different as those of Carthage and Rome, Protestant Holland and Catholic Spain. That view, too, was later to be elaborated by a considerable school of writers. Two separate nations, they declared, had arisen within the United States in 1861, much as two separate nations emerged within the first British Empire by 1776. Contrasting ways of life, rival group consciousness,

---

*We stated in an earlier chapter that Southern leaders in 1857 had time for a few more decisions, but they had to think fast and think straight. This slave-code demand represented their most flagrant error. It has been said that Jefferson Davis adopted it because his blatherskite rival A. G. Brown took it up. But a true statesman does not let an irresponsible rival force him into courses he recognizes as unwise.

divergent hopes and fears made a movement for separation logical; and the minority people, believing its peculiar civilization in danger of suppression, began a war for independence. We are told, indeed, that two types of nationalism came into conflict: a Northern nationalism which wished to preserve the unity of the whole republic, and a Southern nationalism intent on creating an entirely new republic.

It is evident that some of these explanations deal with merely superficial phenomena, and that others, when taken separately, represent but subsidiary elements in the play of forces. Slavery was a great fact; the demands of Northern industrialism constituted a great fact; sectional hysteria was a great fact. But do they not perhaps relate themselves to some profounder underlying cause? This question has inspired one student to suggest that "the confusion of a growing state" may offer the fundamental explanation of the drift to war; an unsatisfactory hypothesis, for westward growth, railroad growth, business growth, and cultural growth, however much attended with "confusion," were unifying factors, and it was not the new-made West but old-settled South Carolina which led in the schism.

One fact needs emphatic statement: of all the monistic explanations for the drift to war, that posited upon supposed economic causes is the flimsiest. This theory was sharply rejected at the time by so astute an observer as Alexander H. Stephens. South Carolina, he wrote his brother on New Year's Day, 1861, was seceding from a tariff "which is just what her own Senators and members in Congress made it." As for the charges of consolidation and despotism made by some Carolinians, he thought they arose from peevishness rather than a calm analysis of facts. "The truth is, the South, almost in mass, has voted, I think, for every measure of general legislation that has passed both houses and become law for the last ten years." The South, far from groaning under tyranny, had controlled the government almost from its beginning, and Stephens believed that its only real grievance lay in the Northern refusal to return fugitive slaves and to stop the antislavery agitation. "All other complaints are founded on threatened dangers which may never come, and which I feel very sure would be averted if the South would pursue a judicious and wise course." Stephens was right. It was true that the whole tendency of Federal legislation 1842–1860 was toward free trade; true that the tariff in force when secession began was largely Southern-made; true that it was the lowest tariff the country had known since 1816; true that it cost a nation of thirty million people but sixty million dollars in indirect revenue; true that without secession no new tariff law, obnoxious to the Democratic Party, could have passed before 1863—if then.

In the official explanations which one Southern State after another published for its secession, economic grievances are either omitted entirely or given minor position. There were few such supposed grievances which the agricultural States of Illinois, Iowa, Indiana, Wisconsin, and Minnesota did not share with the South—and they never threatened to secede. Charles A. Beard finds the tap-root of the war in the resistance of the planter interest to Northern demands enlarging the old Hamilton-Webster policy. The South was adamant in standing for "no high protective tariffs, no ship subsidies, no national banking and currency system; in short, none of the measures which business enterprise deemed essential to its progress." But the Republican platform in 1856 was silent on the tariff; in 1860 it carried a milk-and-water statement on the subject which Western Republicans took, mild as it was, with a wry face; the incoming President was little interested in the tariff; and any harsh legislation was impossible. Ship subsidies were not an issue in the campaign of 1860. Neither were a national banking system and a national currency system. They were not mentioned in the Republican platform nor discussed by party debaters. The Pacific Railroad was advocated both by the Douglas Democrats and the Republicans; and it is noteworthy that Seward and Douglas were for building both a Northern and a Southern line. In short, the divisive economic issues are easily exaggerated. At the same time, the unifying economic factors were both numerous and powerful. North and South had economies which were largely complementary. It was no misfortune to the South that Massachusetts cotton mills wanted its staple, and that New York ironmasters like Hewitt were eager to sell rails dirt-cheap to Southern railway builders; and sober businessmen on both sides, merchants, bankers, and manufacturers, were the men most anxious to keep the peace and hold the Union together.*

We must seek further for an explanation; and in so doing, we must give special weight to the observations of penetrating leaders of the time, who knew at firsthand the spirit of the people. Henry J. Raymond, moderate editor of the New York *Times,* a sagacious man who disliked Northern abolitionists and Southern radicals, wrote in January, 1860, an analysis of the impending conflict which attributed it to a competition for power:

In every country there must be a just and equal balance of powers in the government, an equal distribution of the national forces. Each section and each interest must exercise its due share of influence and control. It is always more or less difficult to preserve their just equipoise, and the larger the country, and the more varied its great interests, the more difficult does the task become, and the greater the shock and disturbance caused by an attempt to adjust it when once disturbed. I believe I state only what is generally conceded to be a fact, when I say that the growth of the Northern States in population, in wealth, in all the elements of political influence and control, has been out of proportion to their political influence in the Federal Councils. While the Southern States have less than a third of the aggregate population of the Union, their interests have influenced the policy of the government far more than the interests of the Northern States. . . . Now the North has made rapid advances within the last five years, and it naturally claims a proportionate share of influence and power in the affairs of the Confederacy.

It is inevitable that this claim should be put forward, and it is also inevitable that it should be conceded. No party can long resist it; it overrides all parties, and makes them the mere instruments of its will. It is quite as strong today in the heart of the Democratic party of the North as in the Republican ranks; and any party which ignores it will lose its hold on the public mind.

Why does the South resist this claim? Not because it is unjust in itself, but because it has become involved with the question of slavery, and has drawn so much of its vigor and vitality from that quarter, that it is almost merged in that issue. The North bases its demand for

---

*South Carolina's Declaration of immediate causes of secession ignored economic issues, and concentrated upon slavery. Rhett's Address to the other slaveholding States did charge the North with gross injustice in tariff legislation; but the whole body of South Carolina's Representatives and Senators had voted for the existing tariff of 1857, and Rhett in defending his Address declared that to win the sympathy of Britain and France, a protest against protective tariffs would be more useful than a protest grounded on the slavery question. McPherson, *Political History,* 12–20.

increased power, in a very great degree, on the action of the government in regard to slavery—and the just and rightful ascendancy of the North in the Federal councils comes thus to be regarded as an element of danger to the institutions of the Southern States.

In brief, Raymond, who held that slavery was a moral wrong, that its economic and social tendencies were vicious, and that the time had come to halt its growth with a view to its final eradication, believed that the contest was primarily one for power, and for the application of that power to the slave system. With this opinion Alexander H. Stephens agreed. The Georgian said he believed slavery both morally and politically right. In his letter to Lincoln on December 30, 1860, he declared that the South did not fear that the new Republican Administration would interfere directly and immediately with slavery in the States. What Southerners did fear was the ultimate result of the shift of power which had just occurred—in its application to slavery:

Now this subject, which is confessedly on all sides outside of the constitutional action of the Government, so far as the States are concerned, is made the 'central idea' in the platform of principles announced by the triumphant party. The leading object seems to be simply, and wantonly, if you please, to put the institutions of nearly half the States under the ban of public opinion and national condemnation. This, upon general principles, is quite enough of itself to arouse a spirit not only of general indignation, but of revolt on the part of the proscribed. Let me illustrate. It is generally conceded by the Republicans even, that Congress cannot interfere with slavery in the States. It is equally conceded that Congress cannot establish any form of religious worship. Now suppose that any one of the present Christian churches or sects prevailed in all the Southern States, but had no existence in any one of the Northern States—under such circumstances

suppose the people of the Northern States should organize a political party, not upon a foreign or domestic policy, but with one leading idea of condemnation of the doctrines and tenets of that particular church, and with an avowed object of preventing its extension into the common Territories, even after the highest judicial tribunal of the land had decided they had no such constitutional power. And suppose that a party so organized should carry a Presidential election. Is it not apparent that a general feeling of resistance to the success, aims, and objects of such a party would necessarily and rightfully ensue?

Raymond and Stephens agreed that the two sections were competing for power; that a momentous transfer of power had just occurred; and that it held fateful consequences because it was involved with the issue of slavery, taking authority from a section which believed slavery moral and healthy, and giving it to a section which held slavery immoral and pernicious. To Stephens this transfer was ground for resuming the ultimate sovereignty of the States. Here we find a somewhat more complex statement of James Ford Rhodes's thesis that the central cause of the Civil War lay in slavery. Here, too, we revert to the assertions of Yancey and Lincoln that the vital conflict was between those who thought slavery right and those who thought it wrong. But this definition we can accept only if we probe a little deeper for a concept which both modifies and enlarges the basic source of perplexity and quarrel.

The main root of the conflict (and there were minor roots) was the problem of slavery *with its complementary problem of race-adjustment;* the main source of the tragedy was the refusal of either section to face these conjoined problems squarely and pay the heavy costs of a peaceful settlement. Had it not been for the difference in race, the slavery issue would have presented no great difficulties. But as the racial gulf existed, the South inarticulately but clearly perceived that elimination of this issue would still leave it the terrible problem of the Negro. Those historians who write that if slavery had simply been left alone it would soon have withered overlook this heavy impediment. The South as a whole in 1846–61 was not moving toward emancipation, but away from it. It was not relaxing the laws which guarded the system, but reinforcing them. It was not ameliorating slavery, but making it harsher and more implacable. The South was further from a just solution of the slavery problem in 1830 than it had been in 1789. It was further from a tenable solution in 1860 than it had been in 1830. Why was it going from bad to worse? Because Southern leaders refused to nerve their people to pay the heavy price of race-adjustment. These leaders never made up their mind to deal with the problem as the progressive temper of civilization demanded. They would not adopt the new outlook which the upward march of mankind required because they saw that the gradual abolition of slavery would bring a measure of political privilege; that political privilege would usher in a measure of economic equality; that on the heels of economic equality would come a rising social status for the Negro. Southern leadership dared not ask the people to pay this price.

A heavy responsibility for the failure of America in this period rests with this Southern leadership, which lacked imagination, ability, and courage. But the North was by no means without its full share, for the North equally refused to give a constructive examination to the central question of slavery as linked with race adjustment. This was because of two principal reasons. Most abolitionists and many other sentimental-minded Northerners simply denied that the problem existed. Regarding all Negroes as white men with dark skins, whom a few years of schooling would bring abreast of the dominant race, they thought that no difficult adjustment was required. A much more numerous body of Northerners would have granted that a great and terrible task of race adjustment existed—but they were reluctant to help shoulder any part of it. Take a million or two million Negroes into the Northern States? Indiana, Illinois, and even Kansas were unwilling to take a single additional person of color. Pay tens of millions to help educate and elevate the colored population? Take even a first step by offering to pay the Southern slaveholders some recompense for a gradual liberation of their human property? No Northern politician dared ask his constituents to make so unpopular a sacrifice. The North, like the South, found it easier to drift blindly toward disaster.

The hope of solving the slavery problem without a civil war rested upon several interrelated factors, of which one merits special emphasis. We have said that the South as a whole was laboring to bolster and stiffen slavery—which was much to its discredit. But it is nevertheless true that slavery was dying all around the edges of its domain; it was steadily decaying in Delaware, Maryland, western Virginia, parts of Kentucky, and Missouri. Much of the harshness of Southern legislation in the period sprang from a sense that slavery was in danger from *internal* weaknesses. In no great time Delaware, Maryland, and Missouri were likely to enter the column of free States; and if they did, reducing the roster to twelve, the doom of the institution would be clearly written. Allied with this factor was the rapid comparative increase of

Northern strength, and the steady knitting of economic, social, and moral ties between the North and West, leaving the South in a position of manifest inferiority. A Southern Confederacy had a fair fighting chance in 1861; by 1880 it would have had very little. If secession could have been postponed by two decades, natural forces might well have placed a solution full in sight. Then, too, the growing pressure of world sentiment must in time have produced its effect. But to point out these considerations is not to suggest that in 1861 a policy of procrastination and appeasement would have done anything but harm. All hope of bringing Southern majority sentiment to a better attitude would have been lost if Lincoln and his party had flinched on the basic issue of the restriction of slavery; for by the seventh decade of nineteenth century history, the time had come when that demand had to be maintained.

While in indicting leadership we obviously indict the public behind the leaders, we must also lay some blame upon a political environment which gave leadership a poor chance. American parties, under the pressure of sectional feeling, worked badly. The government suffered greatly, moreover, from the lack of any adequate planning agency. Congress was not a truly deliberative body, and its committees had not yet learned to do long-range planning. The President might have formulated plans, but he never did. For one reason, no President between Polk and Lincoln had either the ability or the prestige required; for another reason, Fillmore, Pierce, and Buchanan all held that their duty was merely to execute the laws, not to initiate legislation. Had the country possessed a ministerial form of government, the Cabinet in leading the legislature would have been compelled to lay down a program of real

scope concerning slavery. As it was, leadership in Washington was supplied only spasmodically by men like Clay, Douglas, and Crittenden.

And as we have noted, the rigidity of the American system was at this time a grave handicap. Twice, in the fall of 1854 and of 1858, the elections gave a stunning rebuke to the Administration. Under a ministerial system, the old government would probably have gone out and a new one have come in. In 1854, however, Pierce continued to carry on the old policies, and in 1858 Buchanan remained the drearily inept helmsman of the republic. Never in our history were bold, quick planning and a flexible administration of policy more needed; never was the failure to supply them more complete.

Still another element in the tragic chronicle of the time must be mentioned. Much that happens in human affairs is accidental. When a country is guided by true statesmen the role of accident is minimized; when it is not, unforeseen occurrences are numerous and dangerous. In the summer and fall of 1858, as we have seen, the revival of a conservative opposition party in the upper South, devoted to the Union, furnished a real gleam of hope. If this opposition had been given unity and determined leadership, if moderate Southerners had stood firm against the plot of Yancey and others to disrupt the Democratic Party, if Floyd had been vigilant enough to read the warning letter about John Brown and act on it, the situation might even then have been saved. Instead, John Brown's mad raid fell on public opinion like a thunderstroke, exasperating men everywhere and dividing North and South more tragically than ever. The last chance of persuading the South to submit to an essential step, the containment of slavery, was gone.

The war, when it came, was not primarily a conflict over State Rights, although that issue had become involved in it. It was not primarily a war born of economic grievances, although many Southerners had been led to think that they were suffering, or would soon suffer, economic wrongs. It was not a war created by politicians and publicists who fomented hysteric excitement; for while hysteria was important, we have always to ask what basic reasons made possible the propaganda which aroused it. It was not primarily a war about slavery alone, although that institution seemed to many the grand cause. It was a war over slavery *and* the future position of the Negro race in North America. Was the Negro to be allowed, as a result of the shift of power signalized by Lincoln's election, to take the first step toward an ultimate position of general economic, political, and social equality with the white man? Or was he to be held immobile in a degraded, servile position, unchanging for the next hundred years as it had remained essentially unchanged for the hundred years past? These questions were implicit in Lincoln's demand that slavery be placed in a position where the public mind could rest assured of its ultimate extinction.

Evasion by the South, evasion by the North, were no longer possible. The alternatives faced were an unpopular but curative adjustment of the situation by the opposed parties, or a war that would force an adjustment upon the loser. For Americans in 1861, as for many other peoples throughout history, war was easier than wisdom and courage.

CHARLES A. BEARD (1874–1948) was one of America's best known proponents of the economic interpretation of history. After an association with the renowned Europeanist, James Harvey Robinson, with whom he shared an interest in making the past relevant to all phases of modern civilization, he turned to American history. Stressing the underlying economic factors in the origins of the Constitution, the development of Jeffersonian democracy, and the evolution of society in general, he sought to apply the "new history" to the unfolding of institutional patterns in the United States. The following excerpts from *The Rise of American Civilization,* which he wrote in collaboration with his wife, illustrate his point of view of the Civil War as a "Second American Revolution," in which Northern industrial interests overthrew Southern agrarian domination of the Federal government.*

Charles A. Beard

The Approach of
the Second American Revolution

Had the economic systems of the North and the South remained static or changed slowly without effecting immense dislocations in the social structure, the balance of power might have been maintained indefinitely by repeating the compensatory tactics of 1787, 1820, 1833, and 1850; keeping in this manner the inherent antagonisms within the bounds of diplomacy. But nothing was stable in the economy of the United States or in the moral sentiments associated with its diversities.

Within each section of the country, the necessities of the productive system were generating portentous results. The periphery of the industrial vortex of the Northeast was daily enlarging, agriculture in the Northwest was being steadily supplemented by manufacturing, and the area of virgin soil open to exploitation by planters was diminishing with rhythmic regularity—shifting with mechanical precision the weights which statesmen had to adjust in their efforts to maintain the equilibrium of peace. Within each of the three sections also occurred an increasing intensity of social concentration as railways, the telegraph, and the press made travel and communication cheap and almost instantaneous, facilitating the centripetal process that was drawing people of similar economic status and

*Reprinted with permission of The Macmillan Company from *The Rise of American Civilization,* II, pp. 3–13, 35–54, by Charles A. and Mary R. Beard. Copyright 1933 by The Macmillan Company, renewed 1961 by William Beard and Miriam Beard Vagts.

parallel opinions into cooperative activities. Finally the intellectual energies released by accumulating wealth and growing leisure—stimulated by the expansion of the reading public and the literary market—developed with deepened accuracy the word-patterns of the current social persuasions, contributing with galvanic effect to the consolidation of identical groupings.

As the years passed, the planting leaders of Jefferson's agricultural party insisted with mounting fervor that the opposition, first of the Whigs and then of the Republicans, was at bottom an association of interests formed for the purpose of plundering productive management and labor on the land. And with steadfast insistence they declared that in the insatiable greed of their political foes lay the source of the dissensions which were tearing the country asunder.

"There is not a pursuit in which man is engaged (agriculture excepted)," exclaimed Reuben Davis of Mississippi in 1860, "which is not demanding legislative aid to enable it to enlarge its profits and all at the expense of the primary pursuit of man—agriculture. . . . Those interests, having a common purpose of plunder, have united and combined to use the government as the instrument of their operation and have thus virtually converted it into a consolidated empire. Now this combined host of interests stands arrayed against the agricultural states; and this is the reason of the conflict which like an earthquake is shaking our political fabric to its foundation." The furor over slavery is a mere subterfuge to cover other purposes. "Relentless avarice stands firm with its iron heel upon the Constitution." This creature, "incorporated avarice," has chained "the agricultural states to the northern rock" and lives like a vulture

upon their prosperity. It is the effort of Prometheus to burst his manacles that provokes the assault on slavery. "These states struggle like a giant," continued Davis, "and alarm these incorporated interests, lest they may break the chain that binds them to usurpation; and therefore they are making this fierce onslaught upon the slave property of the southern states."

The fact that free-soil advocates waged war only on slavery in the territories was to Jefferson Davis conclusive proof of an underlying conspiracy against agriculture. He professed more respect for the abolitionist than for the free-soiler. The former, he said, is dominated by an honest conviction that slavery is wrong everywhere and that all men ought to be free; the latter does not assail slavery in the states—he merely wishes to abolish it in the territories that are in due course to be admitted to the Union.

With challenging directness, Davis turned upon his opponents in the Senate and charged them with using slavery as a blind to delude the unwary: "What do you propose, gentlemen of the Free-Soil Party? Do you propose to better the condition of the slave? Not at all. What then do you propose? You say you are opposed to the expansion of slavery. . . . Is the slave to be benefited by it? Not at all. It is not humanity that influences you in the position which you now occupy before the country. . . . It is that you may have an opportunity of cheating us that you want to limit slave territory within circumscribed bounds. It is that you may have a majority in the Congress of the United States and convert the Government into an engine of northern aggrandizement. It is that your section may grow in power and prosperity upon treasures unjustly taken from the South, like the vampire bloated and gorged with the blood which it has secretly sucked from its victim . . . You desire to weaken the political power of the southern states; and why? Because you want, by an unjust system of legislation, to promote the industry of the New England states, at the expense of the people of the South and their industry."

Such in the mind of Jefferson Davis, fated to be president of the Confederacy, was the real purpose of the party which sought to prohibit slavery in the territories; that party did not declare slavery to be a moral disease calling for the severe remedy of the surgeon; it merely sought to keep bondage out of the new states as they came into the Union—with one fundamental aim in view, namely, to gain political ascendancy in the government of the United States and fasten upon the country an economic policy that meant the exploitation of the South for the benefit of northern capitalism.

But the planters were after all fighting against the census returns, as the phrase of the day ran current. The amazing growth of northern industries, the rapid extension of railways, the swift expansion of foreign trade to the ends of the earth, the attachment of the farming regions of the West to the centers of manufacture and finance through transportation and credit, the destruction of state consciousness by migration, the alien invasion, the erection of new commonwealths in the Valley of Democracy, the nationalistic drive of interstate commerce, the increase of population in the North, and the southward pressure of the capitalistic glacier all conspired to assure the ultimate triumph of what orators were fond of calling "the free labor system." This was a dynamic thrust far too powerful for planters operating in a limited territory with incompetent labor on soil of diminishing fer-

tility. Those who swept forward with it, exulting in the approaching triumph of machine industry, warned the planters of their ultimate subjection.

To statesmen of the invincible forces recorded in the census returns, the planting opposition was a huge, compact, and self-conscious economic association bent upon political objects—the possession of the government of the United States, the protection of its interests against adverse legislation, dominion over the territories, and enforcement of the national fugitive slave law throughout the length and breadth of the land. No phrase was more often on the lips of northern statesmen than "the slave power." The pages of the Congressional Globe bristled with references to "the slave system" and its influence over the government of the country. But it was left for William H. Seward of New York to describe it with a fullness of familiar knowledge that made his characterization a classic.

Seward knew from experience that a political party was no mere platonic society engaged in discussing abstractions. "A party," he said, "is in one sense a joint stock association, in which those who contribute most direct the action and management of the concern. The slaveholders contributing in an overwhelming proportion to the capital strength of the Democratic party, they necessarily dictate and prescribe its policy. The inevitable caucus system enables them to do this with a show of fairness and justice." This class of slaveholders, consisting of only three hundred and forty-seven thousand persons, Seward went on to say, was spread from the banks of the Delaware to the banks of the Rio Grande; it possessed nearly all the real estate in that section, owned more than three million other "persons" who were denied all civil and political rights, and inhibited "freedom of speech, freedom of press, freedom of the ballot box, freedom of education, freedom of literature, and freedom of popular assemblies. . . . The slaveholding class has become the governing power in each of the slaveholding states and it practically chooses thirty of the sixty-two members of the Senate, ninety of the two hundred and thirty-three members of the House of Representatives, and one hundred and five of the two hundred and ninety-five electors of the President and Vice-President of the United States."

Becoming still more concrete, Seward accused the President of being "a confessed apologist of the slave-property class." Examining the composition of the Senate, he found the slave-owning group in possession of all the important committees. Peering into the House of Representatives he discovered no impregnable bulwark of freedom there. Nor did respect for judicial ermine compel him to spare the Supreme Court. With irony he exclaimed: "How fitting does the proclamation of its opening close with the invocation: 'God save the United States and this honorable court. . . . The court consists of a chief justice and eight associate justices. Of these five were called from slave states and four from free states. The opinions and bias of each of them were carefully considered by the President and Senate when he was appointed. Not one of them was found wanting in soundness of politics, according to the slaveholder's exposition of the Constitution, and those who were called from the free states were even more distinguished in that respect than their brethren from the slaveholding states."

Seward then analyzed the civil service of the national government and could descry not a single person among the thousands employed in the post office, the treasury, and other great departments who was "false to the slaveholding interest." Under the spoils system, the dominion of the slavocracy extended into all branches of the federal administration. "The customs-houses and the public lands pour forth two golden streams—one into the elections to procure votes for the slaveholding class; and the other into the treasury to be enjoyed by those whom it shall see fit to reward with places in the public service." Even in the North, religion, learning, and the press were under the spell of this masterful class, frightened lest they incur its wrath.

Having described the gigantic operating structure of the slavocracy, Seward drew with equal power a picture of the opposing system founded on "free labor." He surveyed the course of economy in the North—the growth of industry, the spread of railways, the swelling tide of European immigration, and the westward roll of free farmers—rounding out the country, knitting it together, bringing "these antagonistic systems" continually into closer contact. Then he uttered those fateful words which startled conservative citizens from Maine to California—words of prophecy which proved to be brutally true—"the irrepressible conflict."

This inexorable clash, he said, was not "accidental, unnecessary, the work of interested or fanatical agitators and therefore ephemeral." No. "It is an irrepressible conflict between opposing and enduring forces." The hopes of those who sought peace by appealing to slave owners to reform themselves were as chaff in a storm. "How long and with what success have you waited already for that reformation? Did any property class ever so reform itself? Did the patricians in old Rome, the noblesse or clergy in France? The landholders in Ireland? The landed aristocracy in England? Does the slaveholding class even seek to beguile you with such a hope? Has it not become rapacious, arrogant, defiant?" All attempts at compromise were "vain and ephemeral." There was accordingly but one supreme task before the people of the United States—the task of confounding and overthrowing "by one decisive blow the betrayers of the Constitution and freedom forever." In uttering this indictment, this prophecy soon to be fulfilled with such appalling accuracy, Seward stepped beyond the bounds of cautious politics and read himself out of the little group of men who were eligible for the Republican nomination in 1860. Frantic efforts to soften his words by explanations and additions could not appease his critics.

Given an irrepressible conflict which could be symbolized in such unmistakable patterns by competent interpreters of opposing factions, a transfer of the issues from the forum to the field, from the conciliation of diplomacy to the decision of arms was bound to come. Each side obdurately bent upon its designs and convinced of its rectitude, by the fulfillment of its wishes precipitated events and effected distributions of power that culminated finally in the tragedy foretold by Seward. Those Democrats who operated on historic knowledge rather than on prophetic insight, recalling how many times the party of Hamilton had been crushed at elections, remembering how the Whigs had never been able to carry the country on a cleancut Webster-Clay program, and counting upon the continued support of a huge array of farmers and mechanics marshaled behind the planters, imagined apparently that politics—viewed as the science of ballot enumeration—could resolve the problems of power raised by the maintenance of the Union.

And in this opinion they were confirmed by the outcome of the presidential campaign in 1852, when the Whigs, with General Winfield Scott, a hero of the Mexican war, at their head, were thoroughly routed by the Democratic candidate, General Franklin Pierce of New Hampshire. Indeed the verdict of the people was almost savage, for Pierce carried every state but four, receiving 254 out of 296 electoral votes. The Free-Soil party that branded slavery as a crime and called for its prohibition in the territories scarcely made a ripple, polling only 156,000 out of more than three million votes, a figure below the record set in the previous campaign.

With the Whigs beaten and the Free-Soilers evidently a dwindling handful of negligible critics, exultant Democrats took possession of the Executive offices and Congress, inspired by a firm belief that their tenure was secure. Having won an overwhelming victory on a definite tariff for revenue and pro-slavery program, they acted as if the party of Hamilton was for all practical purposes as powerless as the little band of abolitionist agitators. At the succeeding election in 1856 they again swept the country—this time with James Buchanan of Pennsylvania as their candidate. Though his triumph was not as magisterial as that of Pierce it was great enough to warrant a conviction that the supremacy of the Democratic party could not be broken at the polls.

During these eight years of tenure, a series of events occurred under Democratic auspices, which clinched the grasp of the planting interest upon the country and produced a correlative consolidation of the opposition. One line of development indicated an indefinite extension of the slave area; another the positive withdrawal of all government support from industrial and commercial enterprise. The first evidence of the new course came in the year immediately following the inauguration of Pierce. In 1854, Congress defiantly repealed the Missouri Compromise and threw open to slavery the vast section of the Louisiana Purchase which had been closed to it by the covenant adopted more than three decades before. On the instant came a rush of slavery champions from Missouri into Kansas determined to bring it into the southern sphere of influence. Not content with the conquest of the forbidden West, filibustering parties under pro-slavery leaders attempted to seize Cuba and Nicaragua and three American ministers abroad flung out to the world a flaming proclamation, known as the "Ostend Manifesto," which declared that the United States would be justified in wresting Cuba from Spain by force—acts of imperial aggression which even the Democratic administration in Washington felt constrained to repudiate.

Crowning the repeal of the Missouri Compromise came two decisions of the Supreme Court giving sanction to the expansion of slavery in America and assuring high protection for that peculiar institution even in the North. In the Dred Scott case decided in March, 1857, Chief Justice Taney declared in effect that the Missouri Compromise had been void from the beginning and that Congress had no power under the Constitution to prohibit slavery in the territories of the United States anywhere at any time. This legal triumph for the planting interest was followed in 1859 by another decision in which the Supreme Court upheld the fugitive slave law and all the drastic procedure provided for its enforcement. To the frightened abolitionists it seemed that only one more step was needed to make freedom unconstitutional throughout the country.

These extraordinary measures on behalf of slavery were accompanied by others that touched far more vitally economic interests in the North. In 1859, the last of the subsidies for trans-Atlantic steamship companies was ordered discontinued by Congress. In 1857, the tariff was again reduced, betraying an unmistakable drift of the nation toward free trade. In support of this action, the representatives of the South and Southwest were almost unanimous and they gathered into their fold a large number of New England congressmen on condition that no material reductions should be made in duties on cotton goods. On the other hand, the Middle States and the West offered a large majority against tariff reduction so that the division was symptomatic.

Immediately after the revenue law went into effect an industrial panic burst upon the country, spreading distress among businessmen and free laborers. While that tempest was running high, the paper money anarchy let loose by the Democrats reached the acme of virulence as the notes of wildcat banks flooded the West and South and financial institutions crashed in every direction, fifty-one failing in Indiana alone within a period of five years. Since all hope of reviving Hamilton's system of finance had been buried, those who believed that a sound currency was essential to national prosperity were driven to the verge of desperation. On top of these economic calamities came Buchanan's veto of the Homestead bill which the impatient agrarians had succeeded in getting through Congress in a compromise form—an act of presidential independence which angered the farmers and mechanics who regarded the national domain as their own inheritance. . . .

From what has just been said it must be apparent that the forces which produced the irrepressible conflict were very complex in nature and yet the momentous struggle has been so often reduced by historians to simple terms that a reëxamination of the traditional thesis has become one of the tasks of the modern age. On the part of northern writers it was long the fashion to declare that slavery was the cause of the conflict between the states. Such for example was the position taken by James Ford Rhodes and made the starting point of his monumental work.

Assuming for the moment that this assertion is correct in a general sense, it will be easily observed even on a superficial investigation that "slavery" was no simple, isolated phenomenon. In itself it was intricate and it had filaments through the whole body economic. It was a labor system, the basis of planting, and the foundation of the southern aristocracy. That aristocracy, in turn, owing to the nature of its economic operations, resorted to public policies that were opposed to capitalism, sought to dominate the federal government, and, with the help of free farmers also engaged in agriculture, did at last dominate it. In the course of that political conquest, all the plans of commerce and industry for federal protection and subvention were overborne. It took more than a finite eye to discern where slavery as an ethical question left off and economics—the struggle over the distribution of wealth—began.

On the other hand, the early historians of the southern school, chagrined by defeat and compelled to face the adverse judgment of brutal fact, made the "rights of states"—something nobler than economics or the enslavement of Negroes—the issue for which the Confederacy fought and bled. That too like slavery seems simple until subjected to a little scrutiny. What is a state? At bottom it is a majority or perhaps a mere plurality of persons engaged in the quest of something supposed to be beneficial, or at all events

not injurious, to the pursuers. And what are rights? Abstract, intangible moral values having neither substance nor form? The party debates over the economic issues of the middle period answer with an emphatic negative. If the southern planters had been content to grant tariffs, bounties, subsidies, and preferences to northern commerce and industry, it is not probable that they would have been molested in their most imperious proclamations of sovereignty.

But their theories and their acts involved interests more ponderable than political rhetoric. They threatened the country with secession first in defying the tariff of abominations and when they did secede thirty years later it was in response to the victory of a tariff and homestead party that proposed nothing more dangerous to slavery itself than the mere exclusion of the institution from the territories. It took more than a finite eye to discern where their opposition to the economic system of Hamilton left off and their affection for the rights of states began. The modern reader tossed about in a contrariety of opinions can only take his bearings by examining a few indubitable realities.

With reference to the popular northern view of the conflict, there stands the stubborn fact that at no time during the long gathering of the storm did Garrison's abolition creed rise to the dignity of a first rate political issue in the North. Nobody but agitators, beneath the contempt of the towering statesmen of the age, ever dared to advocate it. No great political organization even gave it the most casual indorsement.

When the abolitionists launched the Liberty party in the campaign of 1844 to work for emancipation, as we have noted, the voters answered their plea for "the restoration of equality of political rights among men" in a manner that demonstrated the invincible opposition of the American people. Out of more than two and a half million ballots cast in the election, only sixty-five thousand were recorded in favor of the Liberty candidate. That was America's answer to the call for abolition; and the advocates of that policy never again ventured to appeal to the electorate by presenting candidates on such a radical platform.

No other party organized between that time and the clash of arms attempted to do more than demand the exclusion of slavery from the territories and not until the Democrats by repealing the Missouri Compromise threatened to extend slavery throughout the West did any party poll more than a handful of votes on that issue. It is true that Van Buren on a free-soil platform received nearly three hundred thousand votes in 1848 but that was evidently due to personal influence, because his successor on a similar ticket four years afterward dropped into an insignificant place.

Even the Republican party, in the campaign of 1856, coming hard on the act of defiance which swept away the Missouri compact, won little more than one-third the active voters to the cause of restricting the slavery area. When transformed after four more years into a homestead and high tariff party pledged merely to liberty in the territories, the Republicans polled a million votes fewer than the number cast for the opposing factions and rode into power on account of the divided ranks of the enemy. Such was the nation's reply to the anti-slavery agitation from the beginning of the disturbance until the cannon shot at Sumter opened a revolution.

Moreover not a single responsible statesman of the middle period committed himself to the doctrine of immediate and unconditional abolition to be achieved by

independent political action. John Quincy Adams, ousted from the presidency by Jacksonian Democracy but returned to Washington as the Representative of a Massachusetts district in Congress, did declare that it was the duty of every free American to work directly for the abolition of slavery and with uncanny vision foresaw that the knot might be cut with the sword. But Adams was regarded by astute party managers as a foolish and embittered old man and his prophecy as a dangerous delusion.

Practical politicians who felt the iron hand of the planters at Washington—politicians who saw how deeply intertwined with the whole economic order the institution of slavery really was—could discover nothing tangible in immediate and unconditional abolition that appealed to reason or came within the range of common sense. Lincoln was emphatic in assuring the slaveholders that no Republican had ever been detected in any attempt to disturb them. "We must not interfere with the institution of slavery in the states where it exists," he urged, "because the Constitution forbids it and the general welfare does not require us to do so."

Since, therefore, the abolition of slavery never appeared in the platform of any great political party, since the only appeal ever made to the electorate on that issue was scornfully repulsed, since the spokesman of the Republicans emphatically declared that his party never intended to interfere with slavery in the states in any shape or form, it seems reasonable to assume that the institution of slavery was not the fundamental issue during the epoch preceding the bombardment of Fort Sumter.

Nor can it be truthfully said, as southern writers were fond of having it, that a tender and consistent regard for the rights of states and for a strict construction of the Constitution was the prime element in the dispute that long divided the country. As a matter of record, from the foundation of the republic, all factions were for high nationalism or low provincialism upon occasion according to their desires at the moment, according to turns in the balance of power. New England nullified federal law when her commerce was affected by the War of 1812 and came out stanchly for liberty and union, one and inseparable, now and forever, in 1833 when South Carolina attempted to nullify a tariff act. Not long afterward, the legislature of Massachusetts, dreading the overweening strength of the Southwest, protested warmly against the annexation of Texas and resolved that "such an act of admission would have no binding force whatever on the people of Massachusetts."

Equally willing to bend theory to practical considerations, the party of the slavocracy argued that the Constitution was to be strictly and narrowly construed whenever tariff and bank measures were up for debate; but no such piddling concept of the grand document was to be held when a bill providing for the prompt and efficient return of fugitive slaves was on the carpet. Less than twenty years after South Carolina prepared to resist by arms federal officers engaged in collecting customs duties, the champions of slavery and states' rights greeted with applause a fugitive slave law which flouted the precious limitations prescribed in the first ten Amendments to the Constitution—a law which provided for the use of all the powers of the national government to assist masters in getting possession of their elusive property—which denied to the alleged slave, who might perchance be a freeman in spite of his color, the right to have a jury trial or even to testify in his

own behalf. In other words, it was "constitutional" to employ the engines of the federal authority in catching slaves wherever they might be found in any northern community and to ignore utterly the elementary safeguards of liberty plainly and specifically imposed on Congress by language that admitted of no double interpretation.

On this very issue of personal liberty, historic positions on states' rights were again reversed. Following the example of South Carolina on the tariff, Wisconsin resisted the fugitive slave law as an invasion of her reserved rights—as a violation of the Constitution. Alarmed by this action, Chief Justice Taney answered the disobedient state in a ringing judicial decision announcing a high nationalism that would have delighted the heart of John Marshall, informing the recalcitrant Wisconsin that the Constitution and laws enacted under it were supreme; that the fugitive slave law was fully authorized by the Constitution; and that the Supreme Court was the final arbiter in all controversies over the respective powers of the states and the United States. "If such an arbiter had not been provided in our complicated system of government, internal tranquility could not have been preserved and if such controversies were left to the arbitrament of physical force, our Government, State and National, would cease to be a government of laws, and revolution by force of arms would take the place of courts of justice and judicial decisions." No nullification here; no right of a state to judge for itself respecting infractions of the Constitution by the federal government; federal law is binding everywhere and the Supreme Court, a branch of the national government, is the final judge.

And in what language did Wisconsin reply? The legislature of the state, in a solemn resolution, declared that the decision of the Supreme Court of the United States in the case in question was in direct conflict with the Constitution. It vowed that the essential principles of the Kentucky doctrine of nullification were sound. Then it closed with the rebel fling: "that the several states . . . being sovereign and independent, have the unquestionable right to judge of its [the Constitution's] infraction and that a positive defiance by those sovereignties of all unauthorized acts done or attempted to be done under color of that instrument is the rightful remedy."

That was in 1859. Within two years, men who had voted for that resolution and cheered its adoption were marching off in martial array to vindicate on southern battlefields the supremacy of the Union and the sovereignty of the nation. By that fateful hour the southern politicians who had applauded Taney's declaration that the Supreme Court was the final arbiter in controversies between the states and the national government had come to the solemn conclusion that the states themselves were the arbiters. Such words and events being facts, there can be but one judgment in the court of history; namely, that major premises respecting the nature of the Constitution and deductions made logically from them with masterly eloquence were minor factors in the grand dispute as compared with the interests, desires, and passions that lay deep in the hearts and minds of the contestants.

Indeed, honorable men who held diametrically opposite views found warrant for each in the Constitution. All parties and all individuals, save the extreme abolitionists, protested in an unbroken chant their devotion to the national covenant and to the principles and memory of the inspired men who framed it.

As the Bible was sometimes taken as a guide for theologians traveling in opposite directions, so the Constitution was the beacon that lighted the way of statesmen who differed utterly on the issues of the middle period. Again and again Calhoun declared that his one supreme object was to sustain the Constitution in its pristine purity of principle: "to turn back the government," as he said, "to where it commenced its operation in 1789 . . . to take a fresh start, a new departure, on the States Rights Republican tack, as was intended by the framers of the Constitution."

This was the eternal refrain of Calhoun's school. The bank, subsidies to shipping, protection for industries, the encouragement of business enterprise by public assistance were all departures from the Constitution and the intentions of its framers, all contrary to the fundamental compact of the land. This refrain reverberated through Democratic speeches in Congress, the platform of the party, and the official utterances of its statesmen. "The liberal principles embodied by Jefferson in the Declaration of Independence and sanctioned by the Constitution . . . have ever been cardinal principles in the Democratic faith"— such was the characteristic declaration of the elect in every platform after 1840. The Constitution warrants the peaceful secession of states by legal process—such was the answer of Jefferson Davis to those who charged him with raising the flag of revolution. Everything done by the Democratic party while in power was constitutional and finally, as a crowning act of grace, the Constitution gave approval to its own destruction and the dissolution of the Union.

It followed from this line of reasoning as night the day that the measures advanced by the Whigs and later by the

Republicans were unconstitutional. In fact, Calhoun devoted the burden of a great speech in 1839 to showing how everything done by Hamilton and his school was a violation of the Constitution. Party manifestoes reiterated the pronouncements of party statesmen on this point. In their platform of 1840, the Democrats highly resolved that "the Constitution does not confer upon the general government the power . . . to carry on a general system of internal improvement . . . the Constitution does not confer authority upon the federal government, directly or indirectly, to assume the debts of the several states . . . Congress has no power to charter a United States Bank . . . Congress has no power, under the Constitution, to interfere with or control the domestic institutions of the several states." This declaration was repeated every four years substantially in the same form. After the Supreme Court announced in the Dred Scott case that Congress could not prohibit slavery in the territories, the Democratic party added that the doctrine "should be respected by all good citizens and enforced with promptness and fidelity by every branch of the general government."

In the best of all possible worlds everything substantial desired by the Democrats was authorized by the Constitution while everything substantial opposed by them was beyond the boundaries set by the venerable instrument. Hamilton, who helped to draft the Constitution, therefore, did not understand or interpret it correctly; whereas Jefferson, who was in Paris during its formation was the infallible oracle on the intentions of its framers.

On the other hand, the Whigs and then the Republicans were equally prone to find protection under the aegis of the Constitution. Webster in his later years devoted long and eloquent speeches to showing that the Constitution contemplated a perpetual union and that nullification and secession were utterly proscribed by the principles of that instrument. He did not go as far as Calhoun. He did not declare free trade unconstitutional but he did find in the records of history evidence that "the main reason for the adoption of the Constitution" was to give "the general government the power to regulate commerce and trade." A protective tariff was therefore constitutional. Furthermore "it was no more the right than the duty" of Congress "by just discrimination to protect the labor of the American people." The provision of a uniform system of currency was also among "the chief objects" of the Fathers in framing the Constitution. A national bank was not imperatively commanded by the letter of the document but its spirit required Congress to stabilize and make sound the paper currency of the land. In fact Webster thought the Democrats themselves somewhat unconstitutional. "If by democracy," he said, "they mean a conscientious and stern adherence to the Constitution and the government, then I think they have very little claim to it."

In the endless and tangled debates on slavery, the orators of the age also paid the same sincere homage to the Constitution that they had paid when dealing with other economic matters. Southern statesmen on their side never wearied in pointing out the pro-slavery character of the covenant. That instrument, they said, recognized the slave trade by providing that the traffic should not be prohibited for twenty years and by leaving the issue open after that period had elapsed. It made slavery the basis of taxation and representation, "thus preferring and fostering it above all other property, by making it alone, of all property, an element of political power in the union, as well as a source of revenue to the federal government." The Constitution laid a binding obligation upon all states to return fugitive slaves to their masters upon claims made in due course. It guaranteed the states against domestic violence, not overlooking the possibilities of a servile revolt. "Power to abolish, circumscribe, or restrain slavery is withheld but power is granted and the duty is imposed on the federal government to protect and preserve it." The English language could hardly be more explicit.

All this was no accident; it was the outcome of design. "The framers of the Constitution were slave owners or the representatives of slave owners"; the Constitution was the result of a compromise between the North and the South in which slavery was specifically and zealously guarded and secured. Such were the canons of authenticity on the southern side.

This view of the Constitution contained so much sound historical truth that the opposition was forced to strain the imagination in its search for an answer. In an attempt to find lawful warrant for their creed in 1844, the abolitionists made a platform that became one of the prime curiosities in the annals of logic. They announced that the principles of the Declaration of Independence were embraced in the Constitution, that those principles proclaimed freedom, and that the provision of the Constitution relative to the return of fugitive slaves was itself null and void because forsooth common law holds any contract contrary to natural right and morality invalid.

Although the Republicans did not go that far in their defensive romancing, they also asserted, in their platform of 1860, that the principles of the Declaration of Independence were embodied in the Constitution and they claimed that neither Congress nor a state legislature could give legal existence to slavery in any territory of the United States. But there was one slip in this reasoning: the Supreme Court of the United States, with reference to the Dred Scott case, had read in the same oracle that Congress could not deprive any slave owner of his property in the territories and that the abolition of slavery there by Congress was null and void.

Nevertheless, the Republicans neatly evaded this condemnation of their doctrine, by calling it "a dangerous political heresy, at variance with the explicit provisions of that instrument itself, with contemporaneous exposition, and with legislative and judicial precedent." In short, the Republicans entered a dissenting opinion themselves; while it was hardly authentic constitutional law it made an effective appeal to voters—especially those fond of legal proprieties.

Even in their violent disagreement as to the nature of the Union, the contestants with equal fervor invoked the authority of the Constitution to show that secession was lawful or that the perpetuation of the Union was commanded as the case might be. With respect to this problem each party to the conflict had a theory which was finely and logically drawn from pertinent data and given the appearance of soundness by a process of skillful elision and emphasis.

Those who to-day look upon that dispute without rancor must admit that the secessionists had somewhat the better of the rhetorical side of the battle. Their scheme of historicity was simple. The thirteen colonies declared their independence as separate sovereignties; they were recognized by Great Britain in the treaty of peace as thirteen individual states;

when they formed the Articles of Confederation they were careful to declare that "each state retains its sovereignty, freedom, and independence and every power, jurisdiction, and right, which is not by this Confederation expressly delegated to the United States in Congress assembled." These were undeniable facts. Then came the formation of the Constitution. The states elected delegates to the federal convention; the delegates revised the Articles of Confederation; the revision, known as the Constitution, was submitted for approval to the states and finally ratified by state conventions.

Q. E. D., ran the secessionist argument, the sovereign states that entered the compact can by lawful process withdraw from the Union just as sovereign nations may by their own act dissolve a treaty with other foreign powers.

There was, of course, some difficulty in discovering attributes of sovereignty in the new states carved out of the national domain by the surveyors' compass and chain and admitted to the Union under specific constitutional limitations— states that now outnumbered the original thirteen. But the slight hiatus in the argument, which arose from this incongruity, was bridged by the declaration that the subject territories when taken in under the roof were clothed with the sovereignty and independence of the original commonwealths.

The historical brief of those who maintained, on the other hand, that secession was illegal rested in part on an interpretation of the preamble of the Constitution, an interpretation advanced by Webster during his famous debate with Hayne. "It cannot be shown," he said, "that the Constitution is a compact between state governments. The Constitution itself, in its very front, refutes that idea; it declares that it is ordained and established by the people of the United States. . . . It even does not say that it is established by the people of the several states; but pronounces that it is established by the people of the United States in the aggregate." That is, the Constitution was not made by the states; it was made by a high collective sovereign towering above them—the people of the United States.

This fair argument, which seemed convincing on its face, was later demolished by reference to the journals of the Convention that drafted the Constitution. When the preamble was originally drawn, it ran: "We, the people of the states of New Hampshire, Massachusetts, &c., . . . do ordain and establish the following Constitution." But on second thought the framers realized that according to their own decree the new government was to be set up as soon as nine states had ratified the proposed instrument. It was obviously undesirable to enumerate the states of the Union in advance, for some of them might withhold their approval. Therefore the first draft was abandoned and the words "We the people of the United States" substituted. The facts of record accordingly exploded the whole thesis built on this sandy foundation.

This fallacy Lincoln was careful to avoid in his first inaugural address. Seeking a more secure historical basis for his faith, he pointed out that the Union was in fact older than the Constitution, older than the Declaration of Independence. It was formed, he said, by the Articles of Association framed in 1774 by the Continental Congress speaking in the name of revolutionary America. It was matured and continued in the Declaration of Independence which proclaimed "these United Colonies" to be free and independent states. It was sealed by the Articles of Confederation which pledged the thirteen commonwealths to a perpetual Union under that form of government; it was crowned by the Constitution designed to make the Union "more perfect."

Far more effective on the nationalist side was the argument derived through logical processes from the nature of the Constitution itself, by Webster, Lincoln, and the philosophers of their school. It ran in the following vein. The Constitution does not, by express provision or by implication, provide any method by which a state may withdraw from the Union; no such dissolution of the federation was contemplated by the men who drafted and ratified the covenant. The government established by it operates directly on the people, not on states; it is the government of the people, not of states. Moreover the Constitution proclaims to all the world that it and the laws and treaties made in pursuance of its terms, are the supreme law of the land and that the judges of the states are bound thereby, "anything in the constitution and laws of any state to the contrary notwithstanding." Finally, the Supreme Court of the United States is the ultimate arbiter in all controversies arising between the national government and the states. Chief Justice Marshall had proclaimed the doctrine in beating down the resistance of Virginia, Maryland, and Ohio to federal authority; Chief Justice Taney had proclaimed it in paralyzing the opposition of Wisconsin to the fugitive slave law. Such being the grand pledges and principles of the Constitution it followed, to use Lincoln's version, that no state could lawfully withdraw from the Union; secession was insurrectionary or revolutionary according to circumstances.

What now is the verdict of history on these verbal contests? Did the delegates at the Philadelphia convention of 1787 regard themselves as ambassadors of sovereign states entering into a mere treaty of alliance? Did they set down anywhere a pontifical judgment to the effect that any state might on its own motion withdraw from the Union after approving the Constitution? The answer to these questions is in the negative. Had they thought out a logical system of political theory such as Calhoun afterward announced with such precision? If so, they left no record of it to posterity.

What then was the Constitution? It was a plan of government designed to effect certain purposes, specific and general, framed by a small group of citizens, "informed by a conscious solidarity of interests," who, according to all available evidence, intended that government to be supreme over the states and enduring. They were not dominated by any logical scheme such as Calhoun evolved in defending his cause; they were engrossed in making, not breaking, a Union; they made no provision for, and if the testimony of their recorded debates be accepted as conclusive, did not contemplate the withdrawal of the states from the federation by any legal procedure. Surely it was not without significance that James Madison, the father of the Constitution, who lived to see secession threatened in South Carolina, denounced in unmistakable terms the smooth and well-articulated word-pattern of Calhoun, condemning secession as utterly without support in the understandings of the men who made, ratified, and launched the Constitution.

But it may be said that the men of Philadelphia merely drafted the Constitution and that what counts in the premises is the opinions of the voters in the states, who through their delegates ratified the instrument. Did, then, the men who chose the delegates for the state ratifying conventions or the delegates themselves have clearly in mind a concept that made the great document in effect a mere treaty of alliance which could be legally denounced at will by any member? The records in the case give no affirmative answer. What most of them thought is a matter of pure conjecture. Were any of the states sovereign in fact at any time; that is, did any of them assume before the world the attributes and functions of a sovereign nation? Certainly not. Did the whole people in their collective capacity make the Constitution? To ask the question is to answer it; they did not.

When the modern student examines all the verbal disputes over the nature of the Union—the arguments employed by the parties which operated and opposed the federal government between the adoption of the Constitution and the opening of the Civil War—he can hardly do otherwise than conclude that the linguistic devices used first on one side and then on the other were not derived from inherently necessary concepts concerning the intimate essence of the federal system. The roots of the controversy lay elsewhere—in social groupings founded on differences in climate, soil, industries, and labor systems, in divergent social forces, rather than varying degrees of righteousness and wisdom, or what romantic historians call "the magnetism of great personalities.". . .

In the spring of 1861 the full force of the irrepressible conflict burst upon the hesitant and bewildered nation and for four long years the clash of arms filled the land with its brazen clangor. For four long years the anguish, the calamities, and the shocks of the struggle absorbed the energies of the multitudes, blared in the headlines of the newspapers, and loomed impressively in the minds of the men and women who lived and suffered in that age. Naturally, therefore, all who wrote of the conflict used the terms of war. In its records, the government of the United States officially referred to the contest as the War of the Rebellion, thus by implication setting the stigma of treason on those who served under the Stars and Bars. Repudiating this brand and taking for his shield the righteousness of legitimacy, one of the leading southern statesmen, Alexander H. Stephens, in his great history of the conflict, called it the War between the States. This, too, no less than the title chosen by the federal government, is open to objections; apart from the large assumptions involved, it is not strictly accurate for, in the border states, the armed struggle was a guerrilla war and in Virginia the domestic strife ended in the separation of several counties, under the aegis of a new state constitution, as West Virginia. More recently a distinguished historian, Edward Channing, entitled a volume dealing with the period The War for Southern Independence—a characterization which, though fairly precise, suffers a little perhaps from abstraction.

As a matter of fact all these symbols are misleading in that they overemphasize the element of military force in the grand dénouement. War there was unquestionably, immense, wide-sweeping, indubitable, as Carlyle would say. For years the agony of it hung like a pall over the land. And yet with strange swiftness the cloud was lifted and blown away. Merciful grass spread its green mantle over the cruel scars and the gleaming red splotches sank into the hospitable earth.

It was then that the economist and lawyer, looking more calmly on the scene, discovered that the armed conflict had been only one phase of the cataclysm, a transitory phase; that at bottom the so-called Civil War, or the War between the States, in the light of Roman analogy, was a social war, ending in the unquestioned establishment of a new power in the government, making vast changes in the arrangement of classes, in the accumulation and distribution of wealth, in the course of industrial development, and in the Constitution inherited from the Fathers. Merely by the accidents of climate, soil, and geography was it a sectional struggle. If the planting interest had been scattered evenly throughout the industrial region, had there been a horizontal rather than a perpendicular cleavage, the irrepressible conflict would have been resolved by other methods and accompanied by other logical defense mechanisms.

In any event neither accident nor rhetoric should be allowed to obscure the intrinsic character of that struggle. If the operations by which the middle classes of England broke the power of the king and the aristocracy are to be known collectively as the Puritan Revolution, if the series of acts by which the bourgeois and peasants of France overthrew the king, nobility, and clergy is to be called the French Revolution, then accuracy compels us to characterize by the same term the social cataclysm in which the capitalists, laborers, and farmers of the North and West drove from power in the national government the planting aristocracy of the South. Viewed under the light of universal history, the fighting was a fleeting incident; the social revolution was the essential, portentous outcome.

To be sure the battles and campaigns of the epoch are significant to the military strategist; the tragedy and heroism of the contest furnish inspiration to patriots and romance to the makers of epics. But the core of the vortex lay elsewhere. It was in the flowing substance of things limned by statistical reports on finance, commerce, capital, industry, railways, and agriculture, by provisions of constitutional law, and by the pages of statute books—prosaic muniments which show that the so-called civil war was in reality a Second American Revolution and in a strict sense, the First.

The physical combat that punctuated the conflict merely hastened the inevitable. As was remarked at the time, the South was fighting against the census returns—census returns that told of accumulating industrial capital, multiplying captains of industry, expanding railway systems, widening acres tilled by free farmers. Once the planting and the commercial states, as the Fathers with faithful accuracy described them, had been evenly balanced; by 1860 the balance was gone.

WILLIAM APPLEMAN WILLIAMS (1921–   ) is one of the most prominent of modern left-wing historians. Primarily interested in the development of American diplomatic relations, which he has taught at the University of Wisconsin and Oregon State University, he turned to the question of the causation of the Civil War in his book, *The Contours of American History.* Arguing that an exclusive laissez-faire philosophy was fundamental to the antislavery crusade, he tends to downgrade the idealistic motivation of the abolitionists, while presenting a more complicated view of the basic conflict between Northern business, Western agriculture, and Southern slavery than the Beards. Excerpts from *The Contours of American History* follow.*

William Appleman Williams

Commitment to Laissez Faire

Long after it has ceased to be an effective weapon of personal recrimination or political strategy, Americans remain haunted by the Civil War. One is sometimes tempted to conclude that never have so many said so much about the same thing that is redundant or irrelevant. Underlying that persistent involvement is the realization that the war undercuts the popular mythology that America is unique. Only a nation that avoided such a conflict could make a serious claim to being fundamentally different. In accordance with the logic and psychology of myth, therefore, it has become necessary to turn the war itself into something so different, strange, and mystic that it could have happened only to the chosen people.

Whatever the appeals and sublimations of that approach, it seems more pertinent to history as a way of learning to examine the Civil War through the convergence of the three moralities of laissez faire that began in the late 1830s and reached an early climax in the Free Soil movement. As they merged in a consolidated system, the religious, political, and economic ethics were also distilled into a few key symbols. These handholds of thought, discourse, and judgment became the most potent and yet inclusive words of the age: *expansion, antislavery, freedom.* As indicated by their use as early as Jackson's time, as well as by their more formal denotations and connotations, they implied that the integrated value system of laissez faire was almost wholly negative. Freedom was defined as release from restriction. Expansion and antislavery were but the two sides of the coin that bought such liberty. But while the defining of evil is a vital function, it is no more than half the responsibility of any philosophy. Lacking a creative vision of community, laissez faire was weak in an essential respect: it provided no basis upon which to deal with evil in a nonviolent way. Its solutions were persistently aggressive and acquisitive.

For these reasons, the northern critics of the Compromise of 1850 were more influential than the southern extremists whose first fuse sputtered out at the Nashville Convention. While many of these northerners were ostensibly anti-expansionists, their position was in reality far more complex. They favored overseas economic expansion and defined the rest of foreign policy largely in terms of the trans-Mississippi west. Most westerners and eastern would-be capitalists shared the latter part of this outlook, and on the issue all of them were vigorous expansionists. Since that region was in fact America's colonial (i.e., underdeveloped) empire, their view was realistic.

But it was also extremely provocative because it defined the issue in very severe terms: would expansion into the trans-Mississippi west be undertaken within the framework of the Constitution, or would that basic law be rewritten in accordance with the abstract principles of laissez faire? The compromises under which the Constitution was adopted, the clauses of that document pertaining to representation in the Congress (which counted three-fifths of each slave) and the rights of states, and the pattern of legislation, and the decisions of the Supreme Court all pointed to a choice between two ways of handling the western territories. Either

they would be opened to slaveholders as well as nonslaveholders, or the region would be divided into slave and nonslave areas. Southerners were willing to accept either of these solutions. So were a good many northerners.

But the advocates of antislavery laissez faire insisted that no one who did not accept their version of the axioms of laissez faire should be permitted to share the territorial empire. And as far as they were concerned, slavery was a violation of those principles. For them, at any rate, the arrival of the Age of Laissez Nous Faire meant that the Constitution had to be interpreted—that is, rewritten—in the light of this outlook. Since the divergence of opinion ultimately defined *the* question, the basic cause of the Civil War was the *Weltanschauung* of laissez faire. Unwilling to compete within the framework and under the terms of the Constitution, northern antislavery advocates of laissez faire finally undertook to change the rules in the middle of the game—and in the middle of the continent—by denying the south further access to the expanding market place.

In the meantime, from 1851 to 1861, the nation and its politicians fruitlessly sought a way to reconcile laissez faire with the Constitution. But since all their proposals hinged on expansion, they never broke free of the impasse. Seward had the keenest insight into this determining factor. "I cannot exclude the conviction," he concluded as early as 1846, "that the popular passion for territorial aggrandizement is irresistible." Small wonder, therefore, that he later called the struggle between north and south an "irrepressible conflict." Nor is it surprising that most leaders of the decade offered little more than Polk's strategy of balancing the gains between competing expansionist elements. Any more positive approach was almost discredited. One congressman with a sense of history expressed the attitude with great perceptiveness: any efforts to co-ordinate and balance the country's development "should be expunged as a disgrace to the country and to the nineteenth century." President Franklin Pierce vented the same spirit in his inaugural assertion that he would "not be controlled by any timid forebodings of evil from expansion." President James Buchanan put it even more bluntly. "Expansion is in the future the policy of our country, and only cowards fear and oppose it."

Thus the issue became dangerously oversimplified: expansion for whom? Throughout the 1850s, moreover, the debate took place against a backdrop prepared by America's first female primitive artist in words and ideas. *Uncle Tom's Cabin,* Harriet Beecher Stowe's landscape of slavery, was published in March, 1852. Though the form had not really been established (Erastus Beadle launched it in 1860), it might fairly be called the first dime novel. It was a crude, jerky, inaccurate, and violent morality play based on the manipulation of a few type-cast characters in one black-and-white situation.

By populating the south exclusively with evil slaveholders and Negroes, Stowe stereotyped the south as evil. There was nothing of the anxiety and hesitance of the area, let alone its initial propensity to accept the Compromise of 1850. The moral was provided by her misleading picture of the Negro as a man who could in "one generation of education and liberty" take his place in society as a fully matured and developed individual. An application of the principles of laissez faire would enable everyone to live happily ever after. Many southerners thought Stowe no more than a typical emancipated female—"part quack and part cut-throat"

—and initially discounted the importance of the book. But the polemic became a guidebook to an enemy—the south—that had already been defined by the value system of laissez faire as it emerged in the program of the Free Soilers and the generalized antislavery spirit. Perhaps nothing defines the essence of laissez faire quite as well as the parallels between the Jacksonian campaign against the bank and the antislavery agitation. Both were negative. Both defined the enemy in secular moral terms. Both were closely tied to economic objectives. Both lacked any positive program for dealing with the problem. And both were undertaken in the name of expansion and freedom.

Even President Millard Fillmore's administration revealed itself as merely cautious (and a bit pro-northern) instead of fundamentally anti-expansionist. Fillmore allowed Commodore Matthew Perry to write his own militant instructions for opening Japan to American commerce, indicated considerable interest in Hawaii, and refused to sign a temperance pledge guaranteeing Spanish control of Cuba. Having argued in 1829 that expansion was "the *principle* of our institutions," Secretary of State Edward Everett in a more fully developed theory anticipated some features of Charles Darwin's theory of evolution. While overrated by the congressman who called it "the most 'manifest destiny' document that ever emanated from the State Department," Everett's long despatch refusing to guarantee the *status quo* in Cuba was a manifesto for empire. Once out of office, he was less verbose: "The pioneers are on the way; who can tell how far and fast they will travel?"

This vigorous spirit also infused a loose association of expansionists known as the Young Americans. Calling for commercial, territorial, and ideological expansion, they wanted to make the United States the hub of the hemisphere, the crossroads of the world, and the patriarch of global republicanism. Other expansionists followed the same general line on their own initiative. Though they ultimately failed, southerners had significant support from politicians and commercial groups in the northeast and the upper Mississippi Valley in their drive to acquire Cuba. And a similar combination of New Englanders, New Yorkers, and southerners almost turned Nicaragua into a Central American Hawaii; Buchanan even recognized their government before internal dissension and armed attack from other isthmian nations ended the colonizing venture.

Despite such involvement in southward territorial expansion, most northerners were primarily interested in overseas economic expansion, ideological empire, and control of the trans-Mississippi west. Their views won out in the Clayton-Bulwer Treaty of 1854, which facilitated trade developments in Central America while checking further territorial annexations by either Great Britain or the United States. Even so, some southerners supported the commercial push across the Pacific. Their trade interests were reinforced by the idea that such a move would help them hold their own in the territorial west, both directly and as a political *quid pro quo*. The result was a China policy designed for "maintaining order there" so that the nation's great economic opportunities would not become "the prey of European ambition."

Convinced that they were the "only powerful race" on the Pacific, some far-sighted northerners like Perry McDonough Collins and Asa Whitney concentrated on plans whereby "American commercial enterprise [could] penetrate the obscure depths of Northern Asia."

Backed by President Pierce and Senator Seward, and of course the Western Union Company, Collins proposed a telegraph system reaching across to Siberia and thence south to India and west to Paris, Berlin, and London. It was a vision of a vast, global funnel with the spout (and the profits) opening into the Mississippi Valley. Whitney stressed a transcontinental railroad to consolidate the opportunity. "Here we stand forever," he exulted; "we reach out one hand to all Asia, and the other to all Europe, willing for all to enjoy the great blessing we possess . . . but *all* [of them] tributary, and at our will subject to us."

Nor was this an irrelevant flight from reality. Not only were large agricultural surpluses being exported, but by 1860, manufactured goods, including iron, amounted to nearly 20 per cent of America's direct exports. But the south received few benefits from the developing subsidizing of such railroads by cash appropriations and massive land grants (approximately 3.75 million acres in 1850, 35 additional projects between 1852 and 1857, and 174 million acres gross between 1850 and 1871). A Mobile-Chicago connection was the most significant offering to the south, and that came too late to alter the established pattern of east-west routes. Land was acquired for a southern route to the Pacific, but such a gulf-coast transcontinental line was never built, at least not for *that* south.

Whatever their serious internal and sectional differences, the north and the west came to define expansion ever more clearly in terms of an interrelated industrial system based on manufactures and food. Despite Buchanan's defense of it as the policy of the "good neighbor" offering a "helping hand," they opposed his plan to snip off a bit more of northern Mexico while that country was preoccupied with internal difficulties, preferring to encourage overseas revolutions that promised commercial advantages. Seward candidly referred to such governments as "the outworks of our system of politics." "We have a direct interest . . . ," agreed a westerner, "in the benefits of commercial intercourse. . . . All we want is that freedom should have a fair battlefield." . . .

On November 8, 1860, a southern gentlewoman summed it up succinctly. "That settles the hash." Since it did indeed, the reasons are important. In the broadest sense, and speaking as the heirs of the physiocratic forefathers of laissez faire, southerners insisted that the Constitution guaranteed minimum protection against *any* political economy. Its leaders interpreted Lincoln's election quite accurately as the victory of a movement to alter the Constitution and abrogate that compromise, literally in the sense of ending southern expansion, and philosophically in the sense of applying *all* the principles of a political economy in *all* the country. The south was correct about it. Lincoln's election did symbolize the coming to power of a revolutionary coalition.

ARTHUR C. COLE (1886–   ) is a recognized
authority on the antebellum period, whose sympathies,
despite a deep commitment to fairness, lay largely
with the free society of the North. During a fruitful
teaching career which culminated in the chairmanship
of the Department of History at Brooklyn College, he
published significant studies both in political and
cultural history. The best known of these is *The
Irrepressible Conflict,* Volume VII of *A History of
American Life,* edited by Arthur M. Schlesinger and
Dixon Ryan Fox, excerpts from which follow. By
tracing the development of two different civilizations in
the North and South, the author seeks to illustrate those
forces which made for the coming of the war.*

Arthur C. Cole

Two Separate Societies

In the summer of 1850 Americans
looked out upon their country with eyes
that glowed with pride and confidence.
"Manifest destiny" had been realized; the
flag had been borne in triumph to the Rio
Grande and to the Pacific shore. As if to
celebrate this great achievement the
mountains of the Far West had loosed a
mighty stream of gold. Within the vast
empire under the "Stars and Stripes" the
forces of political democracy had won
under Western leadership a mighty victory. The American example had been
enviously cited in the recent revolutionary movements in France, Italy and Germany and, lest others overlook it, the government was soon gratuitously preaching
it to Austria and Spain. The old align-
ment, of East and West, of the complacent
settled communities on the one hand and
the changing and obstreperous frontier
on the other representing to some extent
the antipathy of credits and debts was
still sensed, but less keenly than in Andrew Jackson's time. For thirty years
discerning minds had feared that it might
be supplanted by another cleavage, more
clear and strict, between the slave-planta-
tion culture of the South and the industrial and small-farm culture of the North.
Each had reached a high degree of self-
consciousness and it had seemed that their
interests might be mutually antagonistic,
especially in determining the future of
the new land gained from Mexico and
thus of national control. But moderate

*Reprinted with permission of the Macmillan Company from *The Irrepressible Conflict, 1850–1865,*
by Arthur Charles Cole, pp. 1–2, 33, 99–100, 198, 203–204, 241–242, 257–261, 283–284, 406–407. Copyright 1934
by The Macmillan Company, renewed 1962 by Arthur Charles Cole. (Footnotes omitted).

men, representing the varied propertied interests of the nation, were satisfied that—despite the work of agitators and fire eaters—intelligence, forbearance and sentimental nationalism had surmounted all that difficulty when the legislative items just narrowly passed on their own merits were shortly acquiesced in as a great and "final" compromise that should make for national accord. That this apparently perfect balance, this dualism, could not possibly continue with ideals so disparate and aggressive—in fact, that the house was hopelessly divided and on the verge of schism—this in that Indian summer calm could not be realized. . . .

The most highly organized industries, like the iron mills of Pennsylvania, suffered the worst blows [in the Panic of 1857]. In the agricultural South, on the other hand, prosperity and good prices for cotton continued, with only occasional bank failures and suspensions as reminders of the economic interdependence of the sections. Excellent cotton crops prevailed, exports increased and Negro slaves sold at prices that exceeded all past figures. All this was in marked contrast to the social revolution that seemed to threaten the industrial areas. The proud spokesmen of the South therefore boasted of the superior soundness of the cotton kingdom. "The wealth of the South," announced J. D. B. DeBow, "is permanent and real, that of the North fugitive and fictitious." Yet the census summary of industrial progress at the close of the decade showed no perceptible trace of the temporary breakdown of 1857. . . .

New Englanders often migrated in parties or in well-organized colonies. They first sought their kind in the old Yankee belt along the Great Lakes, thus avoiding the antipathy of critics who charged them

with being "sniveling, hypocritical, rascally, white-livered Yankees" afflicted with "cant, humbug, Pharisaism, bigotry, abolitionism, red republicanism." It was not long, however, before they spread out in all directions, even into lower Illinois, that "land of ignorance, barbarism, and poverty." There the Southern bias of the earlier settlers made them less welcome, but missionary zeal inspired many to carry the torch of freedom to light up the darkness of "Egypt." Migrating New Yorkers, Pennsylvanians, Ohioans, Hoosiers and the rest also played an important part. As in the case of Yankee settlers, the older Eastern influences which they brought with them, far from succumbing to frontier experiences and prejudices, came to make a deep impress upon the new environment. Thus the mingling of peoples aided further in breaking down Western suspicion of the Atlantic Seaboard.

The North-South line of cleavage, on the other hand, grew steadily more rigid. Only a few settlers hailed from the states south of the Ohio River; and these, primarily from Virginia, Tennessee and Kentucky, cherished growing doubts concerning the virtues of slavery. This stream remained insignificant until the oncoming war enlarged the flow, bringing many who felt bitterly resentful toward the South and its institutions. The heart of the South had shifted with the culture of cotton to the Gulf states. A common frontier experience no longer bound these states to those north of the Ohio. The barrier between freedom and slavery was fast becoming more effective than the old mountain barrier between the seaboard and the West. . . .

The "isms" that ravaged the country during the fifties evidenced the growing pains of an adolescent nation. Largely confined to the North, their local critics, like Walt Whitman, were usually willing to concede that they were "significant of a grand upheaval of ideas and reconstruction of many things on new bases." Proud Southerners, on the other hand, rejoiced that the land of chivalry had largely escaped the taint of the fads that were sweeping Yankeedom. In less complacent mood they sounded the tocsin of alarm against vagaries of Yankee fanaticism that found their most portentous expression in a militant abolitionism. . . .

Wealthy Southerners, as has been said, had long furnished a valuable patronage to the Northern resorts. Summer Newport was often referred to as a Southern community; a conservative proslavery atmosphere prevailed in the hotels they patronized and even in the churches they attended. In 1858 Senator Jefferson Davis of Mississippi joined a congenial group of prominent Southerners who regularly sojourned near Portland, Maine. As sectional feeling grew sharper, however, the Southern fire eaters insistently demanded a boycott of Northern resorts. Dixie had mountain and seaside attractions of her own, they pointed out. At the same time sensitive Southerners reported an increasingly rude reception upon Northern visits. "We are treated worse in the North than if we were foreign enemies," lamented the editor of the *Richmond Whig*. "Let us with one accord stay home and spend among our own people."

Under this impetus wealthy planters began to erect summer places at the already popular mineral springs in the Virginia mountains, Fauquier White Sulphur Springs becoming especially fashionable. In 1855 a number of Southerners formed a stock company to develop Southern resorts, particularly a spring at Montgomery, Virginia, a few miles from the Tennessee line, where they hoped to create a "Southern Saratoga." A few years later, a number of small watering places with attractive summer residences grew up along the Gulf coast of Mississippi, a convenient location for inhabitants of New Orleans and for planters of the interior. Thus, as the decade drew to a close, the spirit of sectionalism was invading even the sphere of pleasure and recreation. Formerly, leisure-class Americans from both sections rubbed elbows and learned the lesson of tolerance as they exchanged social courtesies and ideas at Saratoga and Newport. But unobserved by the statesmen, coming events disclosed how badly frayed had become the bonds of fraternal feeling and mutual esteem. . . .

If the American nation had become by 1860, as some friendly foreign visitors admitted, "the most generally educated and intelligent people of the earth," this was due not only to the operation of the rapidly expanding public-school system but also to the less formal intellectual and cultural influences that ramified in almost every direction. Carl Schurz ascribed the high average of intelligence in large part to the fact that "the individual is constantly brought into interested contact with a greater variety of things, and is admitted to active participation in the exercise of functions which in other countries are left to the care of a superior authority."

Less reassuring was the circumstance that the cultural advance of these years was sectional in character. For the most part the South, hampered by its caste system, its undigested mass of poor whites and enslaved blacks, its growing antagonism to the free states, remained unaffected by the new currents of civilization. It did not share in the movement for popular education; it took a negligible part in the lyceum movement; it supported few magazines or publishing houses; it had little of a creative nature to contribute to science, scholarship, letters and the arts. More and more it lived to itself, closed in by tradition and by loyalty to a social institution which it alone in all the civilized world maintained and defended. The widening breach between the sections thus reached beyond political acerbities into the very substance of life itself. . . .

As early as the 1840's two major denominations had split upon the rock of slavery and driven their Southern brethren into independent organization. Only the Roman Catholic Church seemed free from the agitation, although its next of kin, the Protestant Episcopal Church, proud of its conservative spirit, also succeeded in steering a safe noncommittal course. It was an easy matter for churches organized in independent congregations without central legislative bodies to practise the gospel of "no fellowship with slave-holders." Moreover, most Baptist, Congregational and Unitarian churches were controlled by elements unequivocally committed to the gospel of freedom. The Western Unitarian Conference at Alton in 1857 did not allow the certain danger of the secession of the St. Louis delegation to prevent the adoption of a strong antislavery report. It is significant, too, that a group of Quakers of Chester County, Pennsylvania, opposed to the conservative stand of their brethren, formed a yearly meeting of Progressive Friends and undertook the freest discussion not only of slavery but also of war, marriage, prisons, property and other established institutions of the day.

Official spokesmen of the Methodist Episcopal Church North commonly pointed to the record of its earnest but conservative protest against the evil of slavery. On the other hand, probably as many as two hundred thousand slaves were owned by its members. Many zealous antislavery men from Northern conferences demanded that the general rule in regard to slavery be made more drastic so that the church might be freed entirely from its "criminal" connection with the institution. This issue was pressed against a declining opposition until the general conference at Buffalo in 1860 adopted a new rule in which, without excluding slaveholders from its communion, it admonished members "to keep themselves pure from this great evil, and to seek its extirpation by all lawful and Christian means."

While the Old School Presbyterians, true to their traditional conservatism, ignored the slavery question, the New School group continued in the early fifties the tactics of trying to appease the antislavery forces by mild condemnations of slavery. The radical element, however, proposed to refuse fellowship to the slaveholder, a program much too strenuous for the cautious leaders of the church and influential laymen like Cyrus H. McCormick, patron of the Theological Seminary at Chicago. Finally, in 1857 when the general assembly voted strong condemnation of a proslavery report of a Kentucky presbytery, six Southern synods with about two hundred churches and fifteen thousand communicants withdrew. With the opening of the Civil War the Old School Presbyterians of the South organized a separate church of their own.

An especial effort was made in the West to enlist the various missionary agencies under the banner of freedom. An important figure in the controversies that arose was President Jonathan Blanchard of Knox College. Convinced that "the heart of action in the Church" was the missions, he declared that from them "the foul spirit of Slavery must be dislodged before it will be *cast out of the Church.*" Accordingly, beginning in 1847, he led a fight at the annual meetings of the American Board of Commissioners for Foreign Missions in favor of barring slaveholders from the mission churches. These efforts proving fruitless, the Illinois Wesleyan Missionary Conference commended the uncompromising antislavery position of the American Missionary Association and urged affiliation with it instead of the formation of rival societies. President Blanchard showed, however, that even this body permitted membership of slaveholders. Meanwhile antislavery Baptists felt impelled to organize the American Baptist Free Mission Society. As a result a group of extreme opponents of slaveholding fellowship, meeting at Chicago in July, 1852, formed the Free Mission Society for the Northwest. For the same reason the Western Tract Convention was organized in 1859 out of antislavery seceders from the conservative American Tract Society.

Meanwhile the common cause of freedom was tending to break down the denominational barriers that separated the Christian antislavery forces. Deprecating the adoption of expediency as a substitute for the spirit of Christ, the crusaders could not but feel that the slavery issue was of more importance than sectarianism. As a result a Christian Anti-Slavery Convention assembled at Cincinnati in April, 1850; in July, 1851, an even more enthusiastic session of two hundred and fifty delegates met at Chicago with Blanchard in the chair. Though the Christian Anti-Slavery Convention disappeared as the conservative reaction set in, it was revived in October, 1859, as the Northwestern Christian Anti-Slavery Convention. Again Blanchard was a leading figure, calling the assemblage to order and justifying his support of the Republican party.

On less drastic tests of their devotion to human liberty the clergy of the nation spoke out with greater courage. Though ministers were oftentimes silent or apologetic, a strong note of protest sounded from many pulpits at the passage of the fugitive-slave law of 1850. Four years later the clergy burst out in wrath against the Kansas-Nebraska act as an assault on freedom. A memorial signed by five hundred clergymen of the Northwest denounced Douglas for "want of courtesy and reverence toward man and God." Promptly conservative editors and politicians deplored the tendency of churchmen to leave their sacred calling and incite partisan strife. "When ministers enter the arena of politics, and associate themselves with the corrupt and lying hypocrites who lead the black republican party, and utter seditious harangues from the pulpit, they are no longer entitled to that respect that their sacred calling commands," declared the *Signal* of Joliet, Illinois, when four of the local clergy participated prominently in a Republican meeting. Such warnings probably restrained the timid at a time when radical abolitionists were wondering whether the cause of freedom could triumph except upon the ruins of the church. Henry Ward Beecher, a brilliant barometer of popular progressive currents, answered critics by advancing the doctrine that any topic introduced into the pulpit became thereby consecrated. Mock slave auctions at his church vividly dramatized many of the horrors of chattel slavery.

Thus the outbreak of the war found most branches of the Christian faith embroiled by the slavery controversy. As the paramount moral question of the day it was regarded by churchgoers on one side of the Mason and Dixon line predominantly from one angle and by those dwelling on the other side predominantly from another; and both groups of

Christians espoused their convictions with a sense of inner righteousness and high scriptural sanction. However reluctant organized religion may earlier have been to enlist in the sectional strife, it failed to stay the tide of revolt and division when the national crisis appeared. . . .

Lincoln's election, indeed, inaugurated a revolution which played havoc with many existing institutions, political, social and economic. But the brunt of the upheaval fell upon the states that had taken their stand for a static, agrarian civilization in which the institution of chattel slavery held the place of paramount importance. Some Southrons consoled themselves with the thought that they were of the blood of a master race, a noble Norman stock not to be crushed by Northern Puritans of vulgar Saxon origin. They repudiated all thought of brotherhood with the Yankees; this was no fratricidal war but a renewal of the hereditary hostility between the "two races engaged." Let not the "Saxonized maw-worm" bring his taint to the soil of the South. Others, like Senator Wigfall of Texas, accepted as compliment and not reproach the description of their section as a primitive but civilized agricultural community. If, they claimed, it lacked not only a commercial marine, manufacturing and the mechanic arts but also any real cities, literature or even press, it was by choice. In such an atmosphere, of course, the plantation system and the institution of chattel slavery might flourish, although then only with the reins of power in the hands of its ardent exponents and champions. But amid the whirl and rush of modern industrial civilization its doom was certain. . . .

After four years of armed strife neither victor nor vanquished was in a mood to view in perspective the bloody struggle and assess the forces that had produced it. The South, its fields ravaged, its homes in smoking ruins, nursed a "lost cause," and mourned that righteousness had fallen before brute strength. Nor had war, "the avenger," satisfied the holy indignation of the North, for "treason" not only had struck at the foundations of the Union, but had loosed the assassin's knife in the final hour of its triumph. It was difficult to recall that but a decade and a half before Northerners and Southerners had proudly formed parts of the same great people, lying on opposite sides of the boundary between freedom and slavery. Both groups had found it wise to court or pacify the maturing West, but, as the frontier moved ever onward, the free North found it easier to assimilate the Western provinces and, at the same time, to make necessary concessions to their demands. The spirit of democracy and the cause of free land spread their influence over the industrial North. The railroad pushed its iron bands across the country binding together the young commonwealths and the old. The fruits of a new and glowing prosperity were tasted in the great agricultural empire as well as in the Eastern marts of trade and manufacture. The throbbing forces of enlightenment, culture and humanitarian reform spread over the North, while free labor, girding its loins, began to feel its power.

South of the Ohio's murky waters a plantation oligarchy basked contentedly in the waning sun of prosperity. For the few, life was easy and pleasant; culture—measured in terms of a passive leisure-class enjoyment and not in science and the creative arts—was within ready reach. An army of Negro vassals and a dependent white class made obeisance to planter rule, though the white yeomanry stirred restlessly as its opportunities of rising to a share in the plantation régime steadily declined and slave labor threatened to become a fatal incubus upon the back of Dixie. The revolutionary victory in 1860 of the forces that challenged the social institutions of the South severed the last bonds that held the cotton kingdom within the Union. Since the North and the administration that represented it refused to "allow the erring sisters to depart in peace," the issue was staked upon the arbitrament of arms. Workshop, farm, drawing-room, press and pulpit—all the gentle arts of peace were dedicated to the shrine of Mars. In the fiery furnace of war and the crushing defeat of the South the permanence of the Union was welded. Yet dislike, suspicion, fear, remained; the gaping wound lingered. Only when it could be bound up and healed could real peace and happiness come to the nation. Then emerged at length the glories of a modern America.

If Arthur C. Cole stressed the development of two separate civilizations on either side of the Mason-Dixon line from the point of view of the North, FRANK L. OWSLEY (1890–1956), a native of Alabama who for many years was Professor of History at Vanderbilt University and the University of Alabama, chronicled the differences from the vantage point of the South. In the following essay, which he contributed to the compendium written by twelve Southerners under the title, *I'll Take My Stand,* he not only defends his section but emphasizes its agrarian ideals. How does his approach differ from Cole's? To what degree does this selection foreshadow Owsley's later insistence on blaming the war on "egocentric sectionalism," with the North bearing a major portion of the guilt?*

Frank L. Owsley

Southern Agrarianism

What lay behind the bitter sectional quarreling between 1830 and 1860? What made the war which followed this quarreling so deadly? Why the cruel peace that followed war? Why the intellectual conquest of the South? The old answer for these questions and the answer which is yet given by the average Northerner is that the whole struggle from beginning to end was a conflict between light and darkness, between truth and falsehood, between slavery and freedom, between liberty and despotism. This is the ready answer of the Babbitts, who, unfortunately, have obtained much of their information from historians such as James Ford Rhodes and John Bach MacMaster. The Southern historians of the Dunning school, all the third generation "rebel historians," and many of the recent Northern historians reject such an explanation as naïve if nothing else. They have become convinced that slavery as a moral issue is too simple an explanation, and that as one of the many contributing causes of war it needs an explanation which the North has never grasped—in fact, never can grasp until the negro race covers the North as thickly as it does the lower South. They are more inclined to take seriously the Southern championship of state rights in the face of centralization as a cause of the struggle; they see that the protective tariff was as fundamental in the controversy at times as the slavery question, and that the constant

*From Frank Lawrence Owsley, "The Irrepressible Conflict," in Twelve Southerners, *I'll Take My Stand,* pp. 68–91. Copyright 1930 by Harper & Brothers; renewed 1958 by Donald Davidson. Reprinted by permission of Harper & Row, Publishers.

expansion of the United States by the annexation of territories and the constant admission of new states from these territories was a vital factor in producing the Civil War—in short, that the sectional controversies which finally resulted in the Civil War and its aftermath were deep rooted and complex in origin, and that slavery as a moral issue has too long been the red herring dragged across the trail.

Complex though the factors were which finally caused war, they all grew out of two fundamental differences which existed between the two sections: the North was commercial and industrial, and the South was agrarian. The fundamental and passionate ideal for which the South stood and fell was the ideal of an agrarian society. All else, good and bad, revolved around this ideal—the old and accepted manner of life for which Egypt, Greece, Rome, England, and France had stood. History and literature, profane and sacred, twined their tendrils about the cottage and the villa, not the factory.

When America was settled, the tradition of the soil found hospitable root-bed in the Southern colonies, where climate and land combined to multiply the richness of an agrarian economy. All who came to Virginia, Maryland, the Carolinas and Georgia were not gentlemen; in fact, only a few were of the gentry. Most of them were of the yeomanry, and they were from rural England with centuries of country and farm lore and folk memory. Each word, name, sound, had grown from the soil and had behind it sweet memory, stirring adventure, and ofttimes stark tragedy. Thoughts, words, ideas, concepts, life itself, grew from the soil. The environment all pointed toward an endless enjoyment of the fruits of the soil. Jefferson, not visualizing the industrial revolution which whipped up the multiplication of populations and tore their

roots from the soil, dreamed of America, free from England, as a boundless Utopia of farms taking a thousand generations to fill.

Men so loved their life upon the soil that they sought out in literature and history peoples who had lived a similar life, so that they might justify and further stimulate their own concepts of life and perhaps set a high goal for themselves among the great nations which had sprung from the land. The people whom they loved most in the ancient world were the Greeks and the Romans of the early republic. The Greeks did not appeal to them as did the Romans, for they were too inclined to neglect their farms and turn to the sea and to handicraft. But the even-poised and leisurely life of the Greeks, their oratory, their philosophy, their art—especially their architecture—appealed to the South. The Greek tradition became partly grafted upon the Anglo-Saxon and Scotch tradition of life. However, it was the Romans of the early republic, before land speculators and corn laws had driven men from the soil to the city slums, who appealed most powerfully to the South. These Romans were brave, sometimes crude, but open and without guile—unlike the Greeks. They reeked of the soil, of the plow and the spade; they had wrestled with virgin soil and forests; they could build log houses and were closer to many Southerners than even the English gentleman in his moss-covered stone house. It was Cincinnatus, whose hands were rough with guiding the plow, rather than Cato, who wrote about Roman agriculture and lived in a villa, whom Southerners admired the most, though they read and admired Cato as a fine gentleman with liberal ideas about tenants and slaves and a thorough knowledge and love of the soil. The Gracchi appealed to Southerners because the Gracchi were lovers of the soil and died in the attempt to restore the yeomanry to the land.

With the environment of the New World and the traditions of the Old, the South thus became the seat of an agrarian civilization which had strength and promise for a future greatness second to none. The life of the South was leisurely and unhurried for the planter, the yeoman, or the landless tenant. It was a way of life, not a routine of planting and reaping merely for gain. Washington, who rode daily over his farms and counted his horses, cattle, plows, and bushels of corn as carefully as a merchant takes stock of his supplies, inhaled the smell of ripe corn after a rain, nursed his bluegrass sod and shade trees with his own hands, and, when in the field as a soldier or in the city as President of the United States, was homesick at the smell of fresh-plowed earth. He kept vigil with his sick horses and dogs, not as a capitalist who guards his investments, but as one who watches over his friends.

The system of society which developed in the South, then, was close to the soil. It might be organized about the plantation with its wide fields and its slaves and self-sufficiency, or it might center around a small farm, ranging from a fifty-acre to a five-hundred-acre tract, tilled by the owner, undriven by competition, supplied with corn by his own toil and with meat from his own pen or from the fields and forests. The amusements might be the fine balls and house parties of the planter or the three-day break-down dances which David Crockett loved, or horse races, foot races, cock and dog fights, boxing, wrestling, shooting, fighting, logrolling, house raising, or corn-shucking. It might be crude or genteel, but it everywhere was fundamentally alike and natural. The houses were homes, where families lived sufficient and complete within themselves, working together and fighting together. And when death came, they were buried in their own lonely peaceful graveyards, to await doomsday together.

This agrarian society had its own interests, which in almost all respects diverged from the interests of the industrial system of the North. The two sections, North and South, had entered the revolution against the mother country with the full knowledge of the opposing interests of their societies; knowing this difference, they had combined in a loose union under the Articles of Confederation. Finally, they had joined together under the Constitution fully conscious that there were thus united two divergent economic and social systems, two civilizations, in fact. The two sections were evenly balanced in population and in the number of states, so that at the time there was no danger of either section's encroaching upon the interests of the other. This balance was clearly understood. Without it a union would not have been possible. Even with the understanding that the two sections would continue to hold this even balance, the sections were very careful to define and limit the powers of the federal government lest one section with its peculiar interests should get control of the national government and use the powers of that government to exploit the other section. Specific powers were granted the federal government, and all not specifically granted were retained by the states.

But equilibrium was impossible under expansion and growth. One section with its peculiar system of society would at one time or another become dominant and control the national government and either exploit the other section or else fail to exercise the functions of government for its positive benefit. Herein lies the irrepressible conflict, the eternal struggle between the agrarian South and the commercial and industrial North to control the government either in its own interest or, negatively, to prevent the other section from controlling it in its interests. Lincoln and Seward and the radical Republicans clothed the conflict later in robes of morality by making it appear that the "house divided against itself" and the irrepressible conflict which resulted from this division marked a division between slavery and freedom.

Slavery, as we shall see, was part of the agrarian system, but only one element and not an essential one. To say that the irrepressible conflict was between slavery and freedom is either to fail to grasp the nature and magnitude of the conflict, or else to make use of deliberate deception by employing a shibboleth to win the uninformed and unthinking to the support of a sinister undertaking. Rob Roy MacGregor, one of the chief corruptionists of the present-day power lobby, said that the way the power companies crush opposition and win popular support is to pin the word "bolshevik" upon the leaders of those who oppose the power-lobby program. The leaders of the Northern industrial system could win popular support by tagging their opponents as *enemies of liberty*" and themselves as "champions of freedom." This they did. Lincoln was a politician and knew all the tricks of a politician. Seward was a politician and knew every *in* and *out*. This is true of other leaders of the "party of high ideals" which assumed the name of Republican party. Doubtless, Lincoln, Seward, and others were half sincere in their idea of an irrepressible conflict, but their fundamental purpose was to win elections and get their party into power—the party of the industrial North—with an industrial program for business and a sop of free lands for the Western farmer.

The irrepressible conflict, then, was not between slavery and freedom, but between the industrial and commercial civilization of the North and the agrarian civilization of the South. The industrial North demanded a high tariff so as to monopolize the domestic markets, especially the Southern market, for the South, being agrarian, must purchase all manufactured goods. It was an exploitative principle, originated at the expense of the South and for the benefit of the North. After the South realized that it would have little industry of its own, it fought the protective tariff to the point of nullification in South Carolina and almost to the point of dissolving the Union. In this as in other cases Southerners saw that what was good for the North was fatal to the South.

The industrial section demanded a national subsidy for the shipping business and merchant marine, but, as the merchant marine was alien to the Southern agrarian system, the two sections clashed. It was once more an exploitation of one section for the benefit of the other.

The industrial North demanded internal improvements—roads, railroads, canals—at national expense to furnish transportation for its goods to Southern and Western markets which were already hedged around for the benefit of the North by the tariff wall. The South objected to internal improvements at national expense because it had less need of transportation than the North and because the burden would be heavier on the South and the benefits greater for the North—another exploitation of the Southern system. The North favored a government-controlled bank; but as corporate wealth and the quick turnover of money were confined to that section, such an institution would be for the sole benefit, the South believed, of the North. There were many other things of a positive nature which the system of society in the North demanded of the federal government, but those mentioned will illustrate the conflict of interest between North and South.

It is interesting to observe that all the favors thus asked by the North were of doubtful constitutional right, for nowhere in the Constitution were these matters specifically mentioned; it is further significant that all the powers and favors thus far demanded by the North were merely negatived by the South; no substitute was offered. The North was demanding positive action on the part of the federal government, and the South was demanding that no action be taken at all. In fact, it may be stated as a general principle that the agrarian South asked practically nothing of the federal government in domestic legislation. It might be imperialistic in its foreign policy, but its domestic policy was almost entirely negative. Even in the matter of public lands the South favored turning over these lands to the state within which they lay, rather than have them controlled by the federal government.

Had these differences, inherent in agrarian and industrial civilizations, been the only ones, it is obvious that conflict would have been inevitable and that two different political philosophies would have been developed to justify and rationalize the conflict which was foreshadowed in the very nature of the demands of the sections: centralization in the North and state rights in the South. But there was another and deadlier difference. There was the slavery system in the South. Before examining the Southern doctrine of state rights, which was its defense mechanism for its entire system of society rather than, as has been claimed, for slavery alone, let us turn to the slavery problem as one of the elements of conflict between the two sections.

Slavery was no simple question of ethics; it cut across the categories of human thought like a giant question mark. It was a moral, an economic, a religious, a social, a philosophical, and above all a political question. It was no essential part of the agrarian civilization of the South—though the Southerners under attack assumed that it was. Without slavery the economic and social life of the South would have not been radically different. Perhaps the plantation life would not have been as pronounced without it, yet the South would long have remained agricultural— as it still is after sixty-five years of "freedom"! Certainly the South would have developed its political philosophy very much as it did. Yet the slavery question furnished more fuel to sectional conflict and created more bitterness than any or all the other elements of the two groups.

Slavery had been practically forced upon the country by England—over the protest of colonial assemblies. During the eighteenth century it had ceased to be profitable, and colonial moral indignation rose correspondingly. However, when the Revolution came and the Southern colonies gained their independence, they did not free the negroes. The eternal race question had reared itself. Negroes had come into the Southern Colonies in such numbers that people feared for the integrity of the white race. For the negroes were cannibals and barbarians, and therefore dangerous. No white man who had any contact with slavery was willing to free the slaves and allow them to dwell among the whites. Slaves were a peril, at least a risk, but free blacks were considered a menace too great to be hazarded. Even if no race wars occurred, there was dread of being submerged and absorbed by the black race. Accordingly, all slaveholders and non-slaveholders who objected to slavery, objected even more to the presence of the free negro. They argued that the slaves could never be freed unless they could be deported back to Africa or to the West Indies. This conviction became more fervent when the terrifying negro insurrections in Santo Domingo and Hayti destroyed the white population and civilizations almost completely and submerged the remainder under barbarian control. All early abolitionists—which meant most of the Southern people up until around 1800—were abolitionists only on condition of colonization. As a result there were organized many colonization societies, mostly in the South during this period.

But colonization was futile. It was soon realized by all practical slaveholders that the negroes could not be deported successfully. Deportation was cruel and expensive. Few of the black people wished to leave the South. The Southern whites shrugged their shoulders and deplored the necessity of continuing the negroes in bondage as the only alternative to chaos and destruction.

Then the invention of the cotton gin and the opening of the cotton lands in the Southwest, 1810–36, made the negro slave an economic instrument of great advantage. With the aid of the fresh cheap lands and the negro slave vast fortunes were made in a few years. Both North and South having now conceded that emancipation was impossible, the Southern planters made the most of their new cotton kingdom with a fairly easy conscience. They had considered emancipation honestly and fairly and had found it out of the question. Their skirts were clear. Let the blood of slavery rest upon the heads of those who had forced it upon the South.

But the opening of the "cotton kingdom" gave dynamic power to the agrarian section, and new lands were desired by the West and South. The now industrial East saw its interest threatened if the South should colonize the territories to the West, including those gained and to be gained. With the tremendous impetus given to the expansion of the Southern system by the growth of the cotton industry and culture, the North became uneasy and began to show opposition to the continued balance of power. This first became manifest in the struggle which resulted in the Missouri Compromise of 1822. Up to this point the objection to slavery was always tempered by the acknowledgment on the part of the North that the South was a victim of the system of slavery and ought to be sympathized with, rather than the instigator of the system, who ought to be condemned as a criminal.

But in 1831 a voice was raised which was drowned only in the roar of battle in 1861–5. It was the cry of William Lloyd Garrison that slavery was a crime and the slaveholders were criminals. He established the famous *Liberator,* which preached unremitting and ruthless war upon slavery and the slaveholder. He knew no moderation. He had no balance or sense of consequence. His was the typical "radical" mind which demands that things be done at once, which tries to force nature, which wants to tear up by the roots. Although he was completely ignorant of the South and of negro slavery, he dogmatically assumed an omniscient power of judgment over the section and the institution. In the *Liberator* or in the anti-slavery tracts fostered by the anti-slavery societies which he aided or instigated, he set no bounds of accusation and denunciation. The slave master, said Garrison, debauched his women slaves, had children by them, and in turn defiled his own children and sold them into the slave market; the slave plantation was primarily a gigantic harem for the master and his sons. The handsome octaroon coachmen shared the bed of the mistress when the master was away from home, and the daughters were frequently away in some secluded nook to rid themselves of undesirable negro offspring. Ministers of the gospel who owned or sanctioned slavery were included in his sweeping indictment of miscegenation and prostitution. In short, Garrison and the anti-slavery societies which he launched, followed soon by Northern churchmen, stigmatized the South as a black brothel. This was not all! The Southern slaveowners were not merely moral lepers; they were cruel and brooding tyrants, who drove their slaves till they dropped and died, who starved them to save food, let them go cold and almost naked to save clothing, let them dwell in filthy pole pens rather than build them comfortable cottages, beat them unmercifully with leather thongs filled with spikes, dragged cats over their bodies and faces, trailed them with bloodhounds which rent and chewed them,—then sprinkled their wounds with salt and red pepper. Infants were torn from their mothers' breasts and sold to Simon Legrees; families were separated and scattered to the four winds. This brutal treatment of the slaves reacted upon the masters and made them brutal and cruel in their dealings with their fellow whites. Such charges, printed in millions upon millions of pamphlets, were sent out all over the world. Sooner or later, much of it was accepted as true in the North.

In the South this abolition war begot Nat Turner's rebellion, in which negro slaves in Virginia under the leadership of Nat Turner, a freedman, massacred their masters, including women and children. The new situation, in turn, begot a revolution in Southern attitudes. Struck almost out of a clear sky by the Garrisonian blasts and the Nat Turner rebellion, Southern leaders were dazed. They dis-

cussed momentarily the expedient of freeing the slaves, then closed forever their minds upon the subject as too dangerous to undertake. Then came a counter-blast of fierce resentment, denying all accusations. The South threw up a defense mechanism. The ministers searched the Scriptures by day and night and found written, in language which could not be misunderstood, a biblical sanction of slavery. Abraham, Moses, the prophets, Jesus, and the disciples on many occasions had approved slavery. History from its dawn had seen slavery almost everywhere. A scriptural and historical justification was called in to meet the general indictment of the wrongfulness of slavery in the abstract. Partly as a result of this searching of the Scriptures there took place a religious revival in the South, which had tended heretofore to incline to Jeffersonian liberalism of the deistic type. The South became devoutly orthodox and literal in its theology. But the abolitionists were not willing to accept scriptural justification of slavery. There was an attempt to prove the wrongfulness of slavery by the same sacred book, but, finding this impossible, many abolitionists repudiated the Scriptures as of divine origin. Partly as a result, the North lost confidence in orthodoxy and tended to become deistic as the South had been. One could almost hear Puritan New England creaking upon its theological hinges as it swung away from its old position.

But there were philosophers and thinkers at work in the South who would meet the abolitionists upon their own grounds. Hammond, Fitzhugh, John C. Calhoun, Chancellor Harper, Thomas R. Dew, either because they felt that scriptural justification of slavery was inadequate or because they realized the necessity of getting away from the theological grounds in order that they might combat the abolitionists upon common ground, approached slavery from the social and economic standpoint. Their general conclusions were that two races of different culture and color cannot live together on terms of equality. One will dominate or destroy the other. There was no middle ground. It had ever been thus. They contended that the negro was of a backward, inferior race. Certainly his culture was inferior. He must either rule or be ruled. If he ruled, the white race would be destroyed or submerged and its civilization wiped out. For the Southern people there was no choice; the negro must be ruled, and the only way he could be controlled, they believed, was by some form of slavery. In other words, Calhoun, Fitzhugh, and the "philosophers of slavery" justified slavery upon the grounds of the "race question"—which U. B. Phillips has called the theme of Southern history, before and after the Civil War. Aside from the scriptural and social justification, these men defended slavery as an economic necessity. They contended that the culture of rice, tobacco, sugar cane, and especially cotton upon which the world depended could not be carried on without slaves. The South, including the up-country and the mountains, accepted the scriptural justification of slavery, to a great extent. The up-country did not accept the economics of slavery, but slavery, in its aspect as a race question, was universally approved in valleys, plains and mountains. It found, in fact, its strongest supporters among the poor whites and the non-slaveholding small landowners. Their race prejudice and fears were the stronger because they knew nothing of the better side of the negro and regarded him as a vicious and dangerous animal whose freedom meant war to the knife and knife to the death. It was the old fear which we have spoken of, common to all in the days

of the Revolution and in the days when Jefferson and Washington were advocating emancipation only on condition that the freedman be sent from the country. Outside of the common agrarianism of the multitudinous sections of the South which acted as a common tie, the race question which underlay slavery, magnified and aggravated by the abolition crusade, was the hoop of steel which held men together in the South in the great final argument of arms.

This abolition crusade on the part of the North and justification of slavery by the South were principally outside of the realm of politics in the beginning. The abolitionists, in fact, had a tendency to abjure politics and demand "direct action," as some of our recent radicals do. But the leaven soon spread, and slavery became a burning political issue. The political leaders of the North, especially the Whigs, after the dynamic growth of the South in the first quarter of the nineteenth century, became fixed in their determination that the agrarian section should have its metes and bounds definitely limited. Industrialism, which had undergone an even greater development than had cotton-growing, declared that the balance of power between agrarian and industrial sections must go. Because slaveholding was the acid test to whether a state would remain agrarian or become eventually industrial, the Northern leaders wished that no more slave states should be carved from the Western territories. Between 1836, when the annexation of slaveholding Texas was advocated by the South, and 1860, when Lincoln was elected upon a platform which declared that no more territory was open to slavery, the major issues in national politics were the struggles between North and South over the admission or exclusion of slavery from the national territories. That is, it was a question whether the territories would be equally open to both sections or whether the North should have an exclusive right in these territories to found its own states and system and thereby destroy the balance of power and control the federal government in the interest of its own economic and social system. Unfortunately for the South, the leaders of the North were able to borrow the language of the abolitionists and clothed the struggle in a moral garb. It was good politics, it was noble and convenient, to speak of it as a struggle for freedom when it was essentially a struggle for the balance of power.

So to the bitter war of the abolitionists and the bitter resentment of the South was added the fight over the balance of power in the form of the extension of slavery into the common territories.

As it has been suggested, had there not been slavery as an added difference between the agrarian South and industrial North, the two sections would have developed each its own political philosophy to explain and justify its institutions and its demands upon the federal government. The North had interests which demanded positive legislation exploitative of the agrarian South; the South had interests which demanded that the federal government refrain entirely from legislation within its bounds—it demanded only to be let alone. While this conflict of interest was recognized as existing in the days of the Revolution when the first attempt at union was made, it was not until the first government under the Constitution was in power that it received a philosophical statement. In the beginning of Washington's administration two men defined the fundamental principles of the political philosophy of the two societies, Alexander Hamilton for the North and Jefferson for

the South. The one was extreme centralization, the other was extreme decentralization; the one was nationalistic and the other provincial; the first was called Federalism, the other State Rights, but in truth the first should have been called Unitarianism and the second Federalism.

It has been often said that the doctrine of state rights was not sincere, but that it was a defense mechanism to protect slavery (implying that slavery was merely a moral question and the South entirely immoral). But Jefferson was an abolitionist, as nearly all the Southern people were at the time the doctrine was evolved and stated by Jefferson, and Calhoun's extreme doctrine of state sovereignty was fully evolved in South Carolina before the crusade had begun against slavery. However, there is no doubt that the bitter abolition crusade and the political controversies between the two sections between 1836 and 1861 over slavery in the territories gave added strength and exactness to the Southern doctrine. Another thrust has been made at the sincerity of the doctrine of state rights: the principle has been laid down that state rights is a cowardly defense used by the industrial interests to shield themselves against the unfriendly action of a more powerful government. Such examples are noted as the extreme sensitiveness of big business to state rights in the matter of federal child-labor laws, federal control of water power, and prohibition. It is not to be denied that it should be easier for the water-power companies to purchase a state than a national legislature—as the market price of a Comgressman is supposed to be somewhat higher than a mere state legislator (though there are certain well-known purchases of Congressmen which seem to contradict this impression). But observe the other side of the question. Big business has more often taken refuge behind the national government than behind the state. I have only to call attention to the way in which corporations take refuge behind the Fourteenth Amendment to avoid state legislation, to the numberless cases brought before the Supreme Court of the United States by corporations whose charters have been vitiated or nullified by state action, to the refuge sought by the railroads in national protection against the state granger legislation, and to the eternal whine of big business for paternalistic and exploitative legislation such as the tariff, the ship and railroad subsidies. Historically, then, the vested interests of industrialism have not had any great use for state rights. They are the founders of the doctrine of centralization, of the Hamiltonian and Republican principles; they have controlled the Republican party; why should they be unfriendly to their own principles and their own political instrument? They have not been! It may be suggested as a principle that for positive exploitation big business has desired large and sweeping powers for the national government, and that for negative business of defense it will hide behind any cover convenient, whether it be a state or the Fourteenth Amendment. The assertion that state rights was a defense mechanism evolved by slaveowners, for corporations later to hide behind, is inadequate if nothing else.

But state rights was a defense mechanism, and its defensive ramparts were meant by its disciples to protect things far more fundamental and larger than slave property. It was the doctrine of an agrarian society meant in the first place to protect the South as a whole against the encroachments of the industrial and commercial North. By upholding the doctrine of a rigid division of powers between state and nation and the literal interpretation of the Constitution such

legislation as protective tariffs, ship subsidies, national banks, internal improvements at federal expense, would be avoided. It would also protect one part of the South against another. While there were infinite diverging interests between the industrial North and agrarian South which made a doctrine of state rights the only safe bulwark against Northern exploitation and encroachment, there were great regional differences within the South itself which made legislation that was beneficial to one section, harmful to another. One section grew cotton and cane, another tobacco and rice, another produced naval stores and lumber; one had slaves, another had none. To throw all these interests into a hodge-podge under one government would be to sacrifice all the minority interests to the one which was represented by the largest population and body of voters. Even among themselves the agrarians felt their local interests safer in the hands of the state than in the hands of a national government. But this was not the end of the logic of local self-government and regional autonomy. The states in turn, because of diverging interests between the Tidewater and Piedmont areas, allowed a large sweep to county government, and built up a system of representation for both state and federal government which would tend to place legislative power in the hands of economic groups and regions rather than in the hands of the people according to their numbers.

The whole idea then was local self-government, decentralization, so that each region should be able to defend itself against the encroachment of the other regions. It was not a positive doctrine; it did not contemplate a program of exploitative legislation at the expense of other regions. An unmixed agrarian society such as Jefferson and Calhoun had in mind called for no positive program.

Such a society, as Jefferson visualized it, called for only enough government to prevent men from injuring one another. It was by its very nature, a *laissez faire* society, an individualistic society where land, water, and timber were practically free. It only asked to be let alone. State rights, local and regional autonomy, did not make for a uniform, standardized society and government. It took cognizance of the fundamental difference between the agrarian South and West on the one hand and the commerical and growing industrial system of the East on the other; and it still further took note, as we have said, of the regional and local differences within each of these systems. It might not make for a neat and orderly system of government, but this was the price of social and economic freedom, the price of bringing into one Union so many different groups and interests.

The interests pointed out have been largely economic and social. These were not the only interests which the state-rights doctrine was expected to protect from an overbearing and unsympathizing national government. Perhaps the greatest vested interest was "personal liberty," the old Anglo-Saxon principles expressed in the Magna Carta, bill of rights, habeas corpus act, supported in the American Revolution, and engrafted finally in every state constitution of the independent states, as "bills of rights." These bills of rights guaranteed freedom of religion, freedom of speech, of thought, of press, of assembly, right of petition, freedom from arbitrary arrest and imprisonment, right of trial by jury, and prohibited the taking of property without due process of law—guaranteed, in short, the fundamental rights which Jefferson had called the "inalienable rights of man" and Locke and Rousseau had called the "natural rights"—right of life, liberty, property, and the free pursuit of happi-

ness as long as the free pursuit of this object did not encroach upon the pursuit of another's just rights. The famous Virginia and Kentucky Resolutions of 1798–9 had been directed at the violation of these liberties. The Alien and Sedition laws which had been pushed through Congress during the Adams administration had struck at many of these. Under the Sedition Act men had been prosecuted for criticizing the President or members of Congress or judges and had been sent to prison in violation of the Constitutional guarantee of freedom of speech. Opinion had been suppressed, meetings broken up, arbitrary arrests made, men held without trial; in fact, the whole body of personal liberties had been brushed aside by the Federalist or centralizing party eight years after the founding of the present federal system under the Constitution. Jefferson and Madison, supported by the state-rights apostle of Virginia, John Taylor of Caroline, and the irascible old democrat, John Randolph, proclaimed that the federal government had thus shown itself to be an unsafe protector of liberty. So Jefferson announced in his inaugural, which was made possible by the excesses of the centralizing party of the East, that the states were the safest guardians of human liberty and called on all to support "the state governments in all their rights, as the most competent administrations for our domestic concerns and the surest bulwark against antirepublican tendencies." The founder of the party of the agrarian South and West upheld state rights as the safest guardian of the liberties and the domestic interests of the people.

Thus the two sections clashed at every point. Their economic systems and interests conflicted. Their social systems were hostile; their political philosophies growing out of their economic and social systems were as impossible to reconcile as it is to cause two particles of matter to occupy the same space at the same time; and their philosophies of life, growing out of the whole situation in each section, were as two elements in deadly combat. What was food for the one was poison for the other.

When the balance of power was destroyed by the rapid growth of the North, and the destruction of this balance was signalized in the election of Lincoln by a frankly sectional, hostile political party, the South, after a futile effort at obtaining a concession from Lincoln which would partly restore the balance of power, dissolved its partnership with the industrial North.

This struggle between an agrarian and an industrial civilization, then, was the irrepressible conflict, the house divided against itself, which must become according to the doctrine of the industrial section all the one or all the other. It was the doctrine of intolerance, crusading, standardizing alike in industry and in life. The South had to be crushed out; it was in the way; it impeded the progress of the machine. So Juggernaut drove his car across the South.

How "men stumbed into a ghastly war" was the theme of JAMES G. RANDALL (1881–1953) in his 1940 presidential address before the Mississippi Valley Historical Association. Considering war the ultimate evil to be avoided, Randall, for many years Professor of History at the University of Illinois, characterized those whom he held responsible for the failure to prevent armed conflict as "the blundering generation."*

James G. Randall

Human Failure

When one visits a moving picture, or reads Hergesheimer's *Swords and Roses,* which is much the same thing, he may gather the impression that the Civil War, fought in the days before mechanized divisions, aerial bombs, and tanks, was a kind of *chanson de geste* in real life. "The Civil War in America," writes Hergesheimer, "was the last of all wars fought in the grand manner. It was the last romantic war, when army corps fought as individuals and lines of assault . . . charged the visible enemy." "The war created a heroism . . . that clad fact in the splendor of battle flags." Hergesheimer feeds his readers chunks of sombre beauty, winterless climate, air stirred with faint cool music, fine houses, Spanish moss and cypress, trumpet vine and bay blossom, live oaks and linden, bridal wreath, japonica, moonflower, and honeysuckle. In his foreword to "Dear Blanche" he writes: "Here is a book of swords . . . of old-fashioned dark roses. . . . [of] the simpler loveliness of the past." His pages live up to the foreword. He gives dear Blanche "The Rose of Mississippi," "The Lonely Star," "Shadows on the Sea," and "Gold Spurs." Of "Jeb" Stuart he says:

Ladies in Maryland gave him the spurs and ladies wherever he chanced to be gave him the rosebuds. . . . Naturally he was in the cavalry. He was different. . . . [He] wore a brown felt hat . . . with . . . sweeping black plume; . . . his boots in action were heavy, . . . afterwards he changed them for immaculate boots of patent leather worked with gold thread; but he danced as well as fought in his spurs.

---

*J. G. Randall, "The Blundering Generation," *Mississippi Valley Historical Review,* XXVII (1940), pp. 3–28. (Footnotes omitted).

The picture is filled in with red-lined cape, French sabre, yellow sash and tassels, The Bugles Sang Truce, The Dew is on the Blossom, orders given when asleep, animal vitality dancing in brilliant eyes.

Escapists may put what they will between the covers of a book; unfortunately the historian must be a realist. Whatever may be the thrill, or the emotional spree, of treating the Civil War romantically, it may be assumed that this has not been neglected. This paper, therefore, will attempt a very different task, that of weighing some Civil War realities, examining some of the irrational ideas of war "causation," and pondering some aspects of the Civil War mind.

Without stressing that Zeebrugge or Westerplatte or the Karelian Isthmus matched any Civil War exploit, or that aviation is as smart as cavalry, it is sufficient to note a few comparisons. If the World War produced more deaths, the Civil War produced more American deaths. If weapons have become more brutal, at least medicine and sanitation have advanced. One seldom reads of the Civil War in terms of sick and wounded. Medical officers of the sixties repeated the experience of a British medical officer in the Burmese War who advised his commander how to avoid scurvy and was told: "Medical opinions are very good when called for." A Union surgeon at Bull Run reported extreme difficulty in inducing field officers to listen to complaints of disease resulting from foul tents into which fresh air was "seldom if ever" admitted. Because ambulances were on the wrong side of the road, this also at Bull Run, twelve thousand troops had to pass before some of the wounded could be taken to the emergency hospital. Wounded men arriving from the field were thrust into freight cars where they lay on the bare floor without food for a day; numbers died on the road. One of the officers refused hospital admittance to wounded soldiers not of his regiment. Medical supplies were thrown away for want of transportation, injured men were exposed to heavy rain, gangrene resulted from minor wounds.

Romance and glory suggest at least the memory of a name. This implies an identified grave, but after making calculations based upon the official medical history issued by the surgeon general, the student would have to inform dear Blanche, or perhaps Mr. Ripley, that if the surgeon general's figures are right the unknown dead for the Civil War exceeded the number killed in battle! In round numbers there were about 110,000 Union deaths from battle, but the surgeon general reported that in November, 1870, there were 315,555 soldier graves, of which only 172,109 had been identified by name, leaving over 143,000 unidentified graves. The number of soldiers known in the adjutant general's records to have died during the war is much greater than the number identified as to burial or reburial. It must be remembered that the soldier regularly carried no means of identification, that graves of men buried by comrades were marked by hasty devices, that Confederates appropriated Union arms and clothing, that teamsters, refugees, camp followers, or even fugitive slaves might have been buried with soldiers, and that the number reported as killed in action was inaccurate. Yet after making all these allowances, the vast number of the nameless leaves the inquiring mind unsatisfied. It is no more satisfactory to realize that about half the Union army became human waste in one form or another, as dead, disabled, deserted, or imprisoned.

"Jeb" Stuart may have worn gold spurs,

but the common soldier was more familiar with fleas. Sashes may have adorned generals but privates were often in rags. It was reported that one of the army surgeons boarded for an entire winter on Sanitary Commission stores. Camps were dirty, sanitation was faulty, cooking was shiftless. Reporting on one of the hospitals, an inspector referred to a leaky roof, broken glass, dirty stairs, insufficient sanitary facilities, and unclean disgusting beds. The soldier who was brutally struck by a sentry of his own company or who contracted malaria would hardly think of his experience as a thing of romance. Without exposing all the euphemisms that obscure the truth of this subject, it may be noted that the great majority of Union deaths were from causes medically regarded as preventable, leaving aside the cynical assumption that war itself is not preventable. Pneumonia, typhus, cholera, miasmic fever, and the like hardly find their way into the pages of war romance, but they wrought more havoc than bayonets and guns. Where there was danger of infection the rule-of-thumb principle of the Civil War surgeon was to amputate, and from operating tables, such as they were, at Gettysburg, arms and legs were carried away in wagon loads. Marching was hatefully wearisome, desertion was rampant, corruption was rife. Individual injustices of the war were shocking. Some generals got credit that was undeserved, others were broken by false report or slandered by an investigating committee of Congress. The men who languished in prison were several times more numerous than those stopped by bullets. That there was heroism in the war is not doubted, but to thousands the war was as romantic as prison rats and as gallant as typhoid or syphilis.

One does not often speak or read of the war in reality, of its blood and filth, of mutilated flesh, and other revolting things. This restraint is necessary, but it ought to be recognized that the war is not presented when one writes of debates in Congress, of flanking movements, of retreats and advances, of cavalry and infantry, of divisions doing this and brigades doing that. In the sense of full realism war cannot be discussed. The human mind will not stand for it. For the very word "war" the realist would have to substitute some such term as "organized murder" or "human slaughterhouse." In drama as distinguished from melodrama murder often occurs offstage. In most historical accounts, especially military narratives, the war is offstage in that its stench and hideousness do not appear.

With all the recent revisionist studies it is difficult to achieve a full realization of how Lincoln's generation stumbled into a ghastly war, how it blundered during four years of indecisive slaughter, and how the triumph of the Union was spoiled by the manner in which the victory was used. In the hateful results of the war over long decades one finds partisanship at its worst. To see the period as it was is to witness uninspired spectacles of prejudice, error, intolerance, and selfish grasping. The Union army was inefficiently raised, poorly administered, and often badly commanded. In government there was deadlock, cross purpose, and extravagance. One can say that Lincoln was honest, but not that the country was free from corruption during the Lincoln administration. There was cotton plundering, army-contract graft, and speculative greed. Where Lincoln was at his best, where he was moderate, temperate, and far-seeing, he did not carry his party with him. Even those matters dissociated from the war, such as homesteading and railroad extension, came to be marred by exploitation and crooked finance. The period of the Civil War and the era of Jim Fisk and Jay Gould were one and the same generation.

If it was a "needless war," a "repressible conflict," as scholars now believe, then indeed was the generation misled in its unctuous fury. To suppose that the Union could not have been continued or slavery outmoded without the war and without the corrupt concomitants of the war, is hardly an enlightened assumption. If one questions the term "blundering generation," let him inquire how many measures of the time he would wish copied or repeated if the period were to be approached with a clean slate and to be lived again. Most of the measures are held up as things to be avoided. Of course it is not suggested that the generation of the sixties had any copyright on blundering. It is not that democracy was at fault. After all, civil war has not become chronic on these shores, as it has in some nations where politics of force is the rule. One can at least say that the Civil War was exceptional; that may be the best thing that can be said about it. A fuller measure of democracy would probably have prevented the war or at least have mitigated its abuses. To overlook many decades of American democracy and take the Civil War period as its test, would be to give an unfair appraisal. Nor does this probing of blunders involve lack of respect for the human beings of that generation. As individuals we love and admire them, these men and women who look at us from the tin-types and Brady photographs of the sixties, though we may have "malice toward some." The distortions and errors of the time were rather a matter of mass thinking, of social solidification, and of politics.

In the present vogue of psychiatry, individual mental processes and behavior have been elaborately studied. Psychia-try for a nation, however, is still in embryo, though it is much the fashion to have discussions of mass behaviorism, public opinion, pressure groups, thought patterns, and propaganda. Scholars in the field of history tend more and more to speak in terms of culture; this often is represented as a matter of cultural conflict, as of German against Slav, of Japanese against Chinese, and the like. Such concepts were given overemphasis at the meeting of the American Historical Association last December. Historians are doing their age a disservice if these factors of culture are carried over, as they often are, whether by historians or others, into justifications or "explanations" of war. The note of caution here should be a note of honest inquiry. It may be seriously doubted whether war rises from fundamental motives of culture or economics so much as from the lack of cultural restraint or economic inhibition upon militaristic megalomania. Modern wars do not relieve population pressure. Whether wars are needed for economic outlets or for obtaining raw materials is highly doubtful. International trade brings all that. Those who create war throttle the very flow of trade that would promote economic objectives. Where the economy of a nation hinges upon an export market, it may happen that plotters of war in that nation will stupidly kill that market by devices of economic autarchy and then claim that they have to go to war to have trade outlets. It is the same with incoming goods. Of such is the economic argument for war. War makers do not open up economic benefit so much as they stifle it. Their relation to culture is no better than their relation to economy.

There is the word astrology for bogus astronomy and alchemy for false chemistry. Ought there not to be some such word for the economic alchemists of this world? Perhaps it exists in the word autarchy. Is it not in the category of bogus economics, or *ersatz* economics, that one should put those who study war as a matter of trade, supply, resources, needs, and production? As for the Civil War the stretch and span of conscious economic motive was much smaller than the areas or classes of war involvement. Economic diversity offered as much motive for union, in order to have a well rounded nation, as for the kind of economic conflict suggested by secession. One fault of writers who associate war-making with economic advantage is false or defective economics; another is the historical fault. It is surprising how seldom the economic explanation of war has made its case historically, *i.e.* in terms of adequate historical evidence bearing upon those points and those minds where actually the plunge into war occurred. One hears war treated as a matter of culture, but cultural and racial consciousness are as strong in Scandinavia or the Netherlands or Switzerland as in militarist-ridden countries. To make conquest a matter of culture is poor history. It may be the vanquished whose culture survives. Culture is not easily transplanted if force be the method. When war comes by the violence of a few in control and by the stifling of economic and cultural processes, it ill becomes the scholar to add his piping to the cacophonous blare of militaristic propaganda.

War causation tends to be "explained" in terms of great forces. Something elemental is supposed to be at work, be it nationalism, race conflict, or quest for economic advantage. With these forces predicated, the move toward war is alleged to be understandable, to be explained, and therefore to be in some sense reasonable. Thought runs in biological channels and nations are conceived as or-

ganisms. Such thought is not confined to philosophers; it is the commonest of mental patterns. A cartoonist habitually draws a nation as a person. In this manner of thinking Germany does so and so; John Bull takes this or that course, and so on. When thought takes so homely a form it is hardly called a philosophical concept; for that purpose the very same thing would appear under a Greek derivative or Freudian label. However labeled, it may be questioned whether the concept is any better than a poor figure of speech, a defective metaphor which is misleading because it has a degree of truth.

Ruritania—to be no more specific— does so and so in the sense that it has a government, the government acts for the nation, and for political purposes there is no other way in which the country can act. The doubtful part is to infer that there is one directing mind for Ruritania which is the distillation of all the millions of minds. Where government has a bogus quality such an inference is more doubtful than if government has a well grounded or established quality. Give certain conditions of forced leadership and suppressed thought, the oneness of exvcutive action in a nation may in fact represent nothing at all in terms of consolidated will and intent distilled from the whole mass. What passes for mass thought these days is not so much distilled as it is translated from golden plates handed down on some ideological Hill of Cumorah and read through the magic of authoritarian Urim and Thummim. The terrifying fact is that such bogus thought can be manufactured; it can be produced wholesale and distributed at top speed; it can control a nation; it is the shabby mental *ersatz* of an abnormal period.

War-making is too much dignified if it is told in terms of broad national urges, of great German motives, or of compelling

Russian ambitions. When nations stumble into war, or when peoples rub their eyes and find they have been dragged into war, there is at some point a psychopathic case. Omit the element of abnormality, or of bogus leadership, or inordinate ambition for conquest, and diagnosis fails. In the modern scene it fails also if one omits manipulation, dummies, bogeys, false fronts, provocative agents, made-up incidents, frustration of elemental impulses, negation of culture, propaganda that is false in intent, criminal usurpation, and terrorist violence. These are reflections on the present bedeviled age, but their pertinence to the subject at hand is seen in the fact that scholarly discussions in explanation of war on the economic or cultural basis frequently include the Civil War as a supposedly convincing example. The writer doubts seriously whether a consensus of scholars who have competently studied the Civil War would accept either the cultural motive or the economic basis as the effective cause.

If one were to explain how this or that group or individual got into the Civil War, he could rely on no one formula. He would have to make up a series of elements or situations of which the following are only a few that might be mentioned: the despairing plunge, the unmotivated drift, the intruding dilemma, the blasted hope, the self-fulfilling prediction, the push-over, the twisted argument, the frustrated leader, the advocate of rule or ruin, and the reform-your-neighbor prophet. Robert Toombs said he would resist Stephen A. Douglas though he could see "nothing but . . . defeat in the future"; there is your despairing plunge. Young Henry Watterson, a Tennessee antislavery Unionist who fought for the Confederacy, is an example of the unmotivated drift. To many an individual the problem was not to fight with the side whose policies he approved of, but to be associated with the right set. Such an individual motive could not by a process of multiplication become in any reasonable sense a large-group motive. Yet it would be understandable for the individual. Usually in war time individuals have no choice of side, though in the American Civil War they sometimes did, especially on the border. Even where such choice was possible, the going to war by the individual in the sixties was due less to any broad "cause" or motive than to the fact that war existed, so that fighting was the thing to do. The obtaining of soldiers is not a matter of genuine persuasion as to issues. War participation is not a proof of war attitude.

The intruding dilemma was found in the great border and the great upper South where one of two ugly courses had to be chosen, though neither choice made sense in terms of objectives and interests in those broad regions. The self-fulfilling prediction is recognized in the case of those who, having said that war must come, worked powerfully to make it come. The blasted hope, *i.e.* the wish for adjustment instead of butchery, was the experience of most of the people, especially in the border and upper South. The frustrated leader is seen in the Unionist who came to support secession, or in such northerners as Thurlow Weed and William H. Seward who sought compromise and then supported war. The plea that "better terms" could be had out of the Union, which implied a short secession gesture though uttered by determined secessionists, was the crafty argument for secession to be used in addressing Unionists. This might be dubbed the twisted argument. The push-over is seen in the whole strategy of secession leaders by which anti-secession states and Union-loving men were to be dragged in by the accelerated march of events.

These are things which belong as much

to the "explanation" of the Civil War as any broad economic or cultural or elemental factor. It should be remembered how few of the active promoters of secession became leaders of the Confederacy; their place in the drama was in the first act, in the starting of trouble. Nor should sectional preference cause one to forget how large a contribution to Union disaster, and how little to success, was given by northern radicals during the war. Clear thinking would require a distinction between causing the war and getting into the war. Discussion which overlooks this becomes foggy indeed. It was small minorities that caused the war; then the regions and sections got into it. No one seems to have thought of letting the minorities fight it out. Yet writers who descant upon the causation of the war write grandly of vast sections, as if the fact of a section being dragged into the slaughter was the same as the interests of that section being consciously operative in its causation. Here lies one of the chief fallacies of them all.

In writing of human nature in politics Graham Wallas has shown the potent effect of irrational attitudes. He might have found many a Civil War example. None of the "explanations" of the war make sense, if fully analyzed. The war has been "explained" by the choice of a Republican president, by grievances, by sectional economics, by the cultural wish for southern independence, by slavery, or by events at Sumter. But these explanations crack when carefully examined. The election of Lincoln fell so far short of swinging southern sentiment against the Union that secessionists were still unwilling to trust their case to an all-southern convention or to cooperation among southern states. In every election from 1840 to 1852 Lincoln voted for the same candidate for whom many thousands of southerners voted. Lincoln deplored the demise of the Whig party and would have been only too glad to have voted in 1856 for another Harrison, another Taylor, or another Fillmore. Alexander Stephens stated that secessionists did not desire redress of grievances and would obstruct such redress. Prophets of sectional economics left many a southerner unconvinced; it is doubtful how far their arguments extended beyond the sizzling pages of *De-Bow's Review* and the agenda of southern commercial congresses. The tariff was a potential future annoyance rather than an acute grievance in 1860. What existed then was largely a southern tariff law. Practically all tariffs are one-sided. Sectional tariffs in other periods have existed without producing war. Southern independence on broad cultural lines is probably more of a modern thesis than a contemporary motive of sufficient force to have carried the South out of the Union on any cooperative, all-southern basis.

It was no part of the Republican program to smash slavery in the South, nor did the territorial aspect of slavery mean much politically beyond agitation. Southerners cared little about actually taking slaves into existing territories; Republicans cared so little in the opposite sense that they avoided the prohibition of slavery in those territorial laws that were passed with Republican votes in February and March, 1861. Things said of "the South" often failed to apply to southerners, or of "the North" to northerners. Thwarted "Southern rights" were more often a sublimation than a definite entity. "The North" in the militant pre-war sense was largely an abstraction. The Sumter affair was not a cause, but an incident resulting from pre-existing governmental deadlock; Sumter requires explanation, and that explanation carries one back into all the other alleged factors. In contemporary southern comments on Lincoln's course at Sumter one finds not harmony but a jangling of discordant voices. Virginia resented Lincoln's action at Sumter for a reason opposite to that of South Carolina; Virginia's resentment was in the anti-secessionist sense. By no means did all the North agree with Lincoln's course as to Sumter. Had Lincoln evacuated Sumter without an expedition, he would have been supported by five and a half of seven cabinet members, Chase taking a halfway stand and Blair alone taking a positive stand for an expedition. What Lincoln refused as to Sumter was what the United States government had permitted in general as to forts and arsenals in the South. Stronger action than at Sumter was taken by Lincoln at Pickens without southern fireworks. There is no North-versus-South pattern that covers the subject of the forts. Nor is the war itself to be glibly explained in rational North-versus-South terms.

Let one take all the factors — the Sumter maneuver, the election of Lincoln, abolitionism, slavery in Kansas, cultural and economic differences — and it will be seen that only by a kind of false display could any of these issues, or all of them together, be said to have caused the war if one omits the elements of emotional unreason and overbold leadership. If one word or phrase were selected to account for the war, that word would not be slavery, or state-rights, or diverse civilizations. It would have to be such a word as fanaticism (on both sides), or misunderstanding, or perhaps politics. To Graham Wallas misunderstanding and politics are the same thing.

The fundamental or the elemental is often no better than a philosophical will o' the wisp. Why do adventitious things, or glaringly abnormal things, have to be elementally or cosmically accounted for? If, without proving his point, the historian makes war a thing of "inevitable"

economic conflict, or cultural expression, or *Lebensraum*, his generalizations are caught up by others, for it would seem that those historians who do the most generalizing, if they combine effective writing with it, are the ones who are most often quoted. The historian's pronouncements are taken as the statement of laws whether he means them so or not; he is quoted by sociologists, psychologists, behaviorists, misbehaviorists, propagandists, and what not; he becomes a contributor to those "dynamic" masses of ideas, or ideologies, which are among the sorriest plagues of the present age. As to wars, the ones that have not happened are perhaps best to study. Much could be said about such wars. As much could be said in favor of them as of actual wars. Cultural and economic difficulties in wars that have not occurred are highly significant. The notion that you must have war when you have cultural variation, or economic competition, or sectional difference is an unhistorical misconception which it is stupid in historians to promote. Yet some of the misinterpretations of the Civil War have tended to promote it.

What was the mind of America in Lincoln's day? It was human, which means it was partly simian! It was occidental. It was New World. It was American, though one would have to be a Stephen Benét to state what that means. It had somewhat of a sense of humor, though not enough. It was southern, or Yankee, or midwestern, or otherwise sectional. It was the mind of the McGuffey reader, by which a world of ready-made ideas is suggested. It was Victorian; it had inhibitions which today appear as droll as its unrepressed whiskers. It was less mechanized than today, being of the horse-and-buggy age. It was soul-searching. It was Christian and it was chiefly Protestant; yet the one most numerous faith was Catholic. Religiously it was fundamentalist. It was not profoundly philosophical and took with resentment the impact of Darwinism. Though polyglot it was far from cosmopolitan. The soapbox flavor or the backwoods tang was characteristic of its humorists. It was partly conditioned by racial backgrounds, such as the Dutch, German, Irish, Anglo-Saxon, or Scandinavian. It differed in the degrees of its Americanization; there was a staggering at variant distances from immigrant ancestors. Often the recent immigrant, such as the German or Scandinavian, took American democracy with more simple faith than the seasoned American. When disillusion came to such, it came hard.

The mind of the time was many things socially, being of the four hundred if one considers the De Peysters and Van Courtlands, or Boston Brahmin, or mountaineer, or of the numerous small farmer group, or of the unvocal laboring class. If one were to have searched for class consciousness in this age, it would have been found less among underprivileged masses than among the aristocrats, the planters, the capitalists; it was they who were indeed class-conscious. Such a matter as the southern gentleman's conventionalized code of honor, including the *code duello,* was a bulwark of exclusiveness and a deliberate social barrier.

As to its war attitude, the mind of Lincoln's day was in part a mind during war, in part pro-war, in part anti-war, in part merely at war. Where it was pro-war it was not necessarily militaristic. Where it was German it was usually not Prussian, being spiritually closer to Weimar or Frankfort-on-Main. What is meant here are minds that were more or less genuine; this would rule out the politician whose mind was usually a synthetic affair made up for the vote-getting occasion. The mind of the time was often the product of intra-American migration. Thus it was Virginia or Kentucky in Illinois, Tennessee in Missouri, Vermont in Indiana, Massachusetts or upstate New York in Ohio. Rural areas had contributed more to these migrations than cities; not much relief of urban congestion had come by way of the westward movement. Perhaps predominantly the mind of America was rural. Yet hardly at all was it a peasant mind, much less proletarian. Never would its educated people have called themselves the intelligentsia. To refer to its middle class as bourgeois would be to use a non-American concept. The middle class did not function as a set social type or bloc.

It would be of interest to examine this mind in segments, but they would have to be complex segments. There would be the American-Victorian-New York élite mind, the midwest-German-farmer mind, the Irish-Tammany-Eastside mind, the immigrant-labor mind, the old American frontier mind, and so on. Quite generally it was three things: Victorian, restless, and habituated to politician-like thinking. The puritanical Victorianism of the age combined with financial imperatives when one of Jay Cooke's cashiers committed the astounding indiscretion of driving a four-in-hand in Central Park on a Sunday afternoon. Cooke warned him that if that were known "amongst financial People" it would bring "great discredit to the Bank." "Credit," he admonished, "is a tender plant." Its delicate growth would be affected by "such a stupid display as a four-in-hand." Business men who did not walk the straight and narrow were "under suspicion." Wall Street was an uplifting factor. Sabbath observance had its Bradstreet rating. Yet it may have been the appearance of evil that was detrimental, for corruption was rampant and social disapproval by no means always attached to methods of questionable financial dealing. Graft and special privilege were respectable. Many a fortune of Civil War origin belonged to the ill-gotten class. Defrauding the government did not make one a social pariah.

In spite of much nobility of sentiment, the Civil War mind seems a sorry *melange* of party bile, crisis melodrama, inflated eloquence, unreason, religious fury, self-righteousness, unctuous self-deception, and hate. Bad party feeling was evident when Seward appeared in the Senate on January 9, 1860, "& not a man from the democracy save Douglas . . . came to greet him." "D——n their impudence," was the comment of William P. Fessenden. Yet this was more than a year before the war opened. It was a time of crisis psychosis. Men felt they were living in great days. The generation had its self-consciousness of mission and destiny. Even the private soldier filled his letters with exalted talk. At the beginning of the war a Massachusetts soldier, telling of a rail journey from Boston to New York, wrote: "Refreshments were lavished upon us . . . cannon sent their boom over hill and dale and bells peeled [*sic*] their tocsin of warning . . . that our train was approaching bearing a Regiment of brave hearts to the defence of our country's capitol [*sic*]." Passing the "Constitution" he wrote: "May they [the colors] ever float over that notable ship . . . as she rides proudly upon the waters of the Union." This proudly riding epistle was but a soldier's letter to his brother. Similar attitudes were characteristic of the South; Mrs. Chesnut referred to "the high-flown style which of late seems to have gotten into the very air."

What the war did to the mind of Ralph Waldo Emerson deserves careful study, though here it can be only hinted. To the

Emerson of the sixties New England was the custodian of sense and elegance, Boston superiority was axiomatic, the South was boorish as well as wicked, and John Brown, well-known in Concord, was a martyr. There are "crises which demand nations," he thought, and a generation might well perish to insure a better life for generations that follow. "What a healthy tone exists!" he wrote in May, 1861. To Emerson not merely *the war* but *war* was an elemental, purifying force. Ridiculing the sentimentalist, demanding that the North must conquer as a matter of culture, he wrote grandly of a strong wind, of "one energetic mind" where there had been "incapacity to move," of war as a searcher of character. War to Emerson was a "dynamometer," taking the fop in the street, the beau at the ball, and lifting them up by something "in the air." "A civil war," he naively wrote, "sweeps away all the false issues." "This revolution," he said, "is the work of no man, but the effervescence of Nature." Reaching almost Nietzschean ecstacy, he burbled: "War is a realist, shatters everything flimsy and shifty, sets aside all false issues . . . breaks through all that is not real." "On with the war" might have been his slogan. "Let it search," he said, "let it grind, let it overturn, and . . . when it finds no more fuel, it burns out."

To illustrate the benefit of war he looked for a simile and found it in the cholera! On this theme he wrote: "We watch its course [that of the war] as we did the cholera, which . . . took only the susceptible, set its seal on every putrid spot . . . followed the limestone, and left the granite." What to David Starr Jordan was an annihilator of the finest and of potential descendants of those best fit to reproduce, was to Emerson a beneficial cosmic force finding its origin in the motion of the planets. Norman Angell's great illusion counted its mental victims among those who passed for philosophers.

When philosophers turned war mongers it was not to be expected that pacifists would have a hearing. The broad cause of peace was one of the casualties of war. In its antebellum background the peace crusade in America was a small affair of humanitarian groups with variant attitudes. It embraced men of intelligent idealism, but its efforts never bore fruit as did other crusades such as that of Dorothea Dix for the neglected insane or of Horace Mann for public elementary education. The Peace Society, launched with the impetus of Christian evangelism by William Ladd in 1828, and promoted by Elihu Burritt and other choice spirits, was thirty-three years old when the guns spoke at Sumter. In those years the society had not been idle. It had made use of the familiar techniques of agitation: lectures, local agents, local chapters, tracts, prize essays, magazines, books, national congresses, and petitions to the seat of government. A vigorous literature was produced, world peace congresses were held, arguments against war were marshalled, arbitration among nations urged, and disarmament advocated. Diverse elements were enlisted, such as Quakers, insurance men, free-traders, and merchants.

Pacifism of the early nineteenth century differed from that of the twentieth chiefly in this, that it was economically and socially conservative. Peace agitation was a matter of Christian evangelism and of social stability. It drew more from the Gospel than from fundamental philosophy. Its swing was to the right rather than the left. It did not march with socialism. It contained sectional trouble-makers in its ranks. Christian and conservative as it was, it often met opposition or at least non-cooperation from ordained ministers. Taking a stand against war was diffi-

cult and complex. Questions arose touching the duty of fighting a defensive war or concerning the right of revolution. To favor peace in the sense of having governments avoid the outbreak of war was very different from avoiding individual participation once war had broken out. Organized peace men were chiefly northerners, rather northeasterners, and the movement was interlocked with collateral movements, especially antislavery. Peace advocacy might or might not mean nonresistance. Not all peace men could accept Garrison's formula of doing nothing to preserve the Union against armed secession.

When war came and as the struggle dragged on, demands for peace were regarded as a kind of defeatism, of surrender to forces which northern idealists considered destructive and evil. Peace became a matter of politics, of anti-Lincoln agitation, of what was called Copperhead disloyalty. Forces that stood outwardly for Christianity denounced it the loudest. Though praising Seward's peace efforts before Sumter, the Peace Society formulated its war-time position after Sumter as follows: "*Peace is always loyal. . . .* We cannot . . . tolerate rebellion. . . . The cause of Peace was never meant to meet such a crisis as is now upon us." The society was a negligible thing; indeed one could read many tomes of American history without seeing it mentioned. It did not associate itself with opposition to the war powers, with anti-Lincoln demands for civil rights, with Vallandigham partisanship, nor with obstruction of the draft. It never made enough of a stir to become notorious. It did not arouse the horrendous and vindictive ire of any Dies committee. Many of its members preferred war to the continuance of slavery; others preferred war to disunion; still others deemed human slaughter not too high a price for ascendancy of a favorite party.

Denunciation of war easily became denunciation of rebellion; this readily passed over into a demand to put down rebellion. The cause of peace as a crusade found a new orientation when war actually existed, for non-resistance could not stop the torrent. It was the dilemma of the pacifist. When peace men face an existing war begun by what they consider an aggressor, their attachment to peace becomes outraged indignation against those who, in their opinion, have broken the peace. Such a feeling is consistent with the motive of stopping the war maker. It is only the cynic who would laugh at the discomfiture of the pacifist when once war exists and when the choice of peace is no longer open. The self-contradiction belongs to those who would put the label of war monger upon peace-time efforts to implement international cooperation and to buttress war prevention. The inconsistency is in misapplying the term "peace bloc" to those isolationist groups which have worked to frustrate international security by way of peaceful organization among nations.

For the Civil War generation the problem of the advocate of peace was only in a limited sense the problem of the conscientious objector. Objectors in the Lincoln period were chiefly associated with established anti-war creeds of religious groups. General objectors on other than religious grounds were not much in evidence. In this the Civil War presented a contrast to the World War, wherein refusal to fight was associated not only with specific Quaker-like groups but with broad liberal attitudes. In both wars the mass effect of organized religion was the opposite of pacifist. In each war administrative authorities of the United States respected the idealism of the objector and gave him the alternative of noncombatant service. In the World War more objectors were relieved than imprisoned, though the imprisoned received the most attention. Imprisonment of objectors as such was not a Civil War practice.

If the pacifist had a dilemma, so did the government. The sincere and serene Christianity of the Quakers could not but command respect, and those who stood their ground were, as a rule, honorably excused from fighting. In the Civil War this leniency was at first an administrative adjustment in a situation where the objector might have expected severe treatment; late in the war it was a matter of statutory amendment to the conscription act. As originally passed the Conscription Act of 1863 did not even exempt ministers. For the objector to stand his ground in early Civil War days meant defiance of the government; the government was demanding a service which the objector refused; leniency was an afterthought. Non-resistance was a Quaker tenet, but here the Quakers, or rather the strictest of them, would have to resist, as did Cyrus Pringle of Vermont, unless their government would make a concession which in such cases it did make. No government can be completely unbending. Government is, after all, an art, perhaps a compromise. If the objector remained obdurate, either the government had to withdraw somewhat from the principle of compulsory military service or a man would be punished for being a Christian. The government took an attitude toward Quakers which it could not take toward all, if conscription were its principle. The Quaker came through the dilemma with less compromise than the government.

It is not of record that Lincoln's Cabinet contained a "minister of national enlightenment and propaganda"; yet propaganda itself was not lacking. In the public "enlightenment" of that time there was boasting, there was rumor, there were atrocity tales, and there was falsehood. Atrocity stories were found not only in newspapers but in congressional reports. There were circumstantial accounts of Confederates bayoneting wounded captives, kicking heads about like footballs, insulting women, and engaging in gruesome tortures. William B. Hesseltine has shown that anti-southern horror tales were not without governmental inspiration in the North and that the secretary of war, the surgeon general, and the committee on the conduct of the war took pains to spread tales of the sufferings of northern prisoners in the South. Motives were various: tales might be spread to carry forward the abolitionist's denunciation of southern cruelty, to satisfy the moral sense by besmirching the foe, or to discourage surrender into southern hands. When the backfire came and these atrocity stories led to questions as to why prisoners were not exchanged, it became necessary to invent the tale that exchange had been stopped by a vicious South intent upon destroying the lives of prisoners. Even the humanitarian motive promoted atrocity tales, and the report of the Sanitary Commission on this subject in no way fell short of governmental accounts.

Lincoln's attitude on such matters was expressed in a speech delivered at a Sanitary Fair in Baltimore in 1864. Referring to the rumored massacre of colored prisoners at Fort Pillow, Lincoln carefully avoided pointing up the reputed atrocity, declared that the event was not known to have occurred, and promised an investigation. He also promised retribution if needed, but, as in the case of similar threats by the Confederacy, the motive was humanitarian. The threat of retaliation was intended to make actual retaliation unnecessary, as well as to satisfy that type of vindictiveness at the North which was strangely bound up with humanitarianism. On this point Lincoln reached the height of caution when he said: "It will be a matter of grave consideration in what exact course to apply the retribution." What seemed to worry Lincoln was not a vicious South, but the need to satisfy his own northern public, including the humanitarianly vindictive public. For the latter he gave a threat of retribution which in fact he never carried out, and probably never intended to.

In spite of its lack of modern techniques such as radio and the movies, Civil War propaganda found many devices. There were drawings in *Harper's*, *Leslie's*, and *Vanity Fair*, though not daily cartoons. There were popular songs such as "Father Abraham" which gave the chief a nickname and personified the cause in a benevolent President. There was recruiting propaganda by poster and otherwise, and there was partisanly patriotic propaganda in appeals for soldier votes. Generals of the political variety made flourishing speeches. The Loyal Publication Society sent out its material by the bushel, including stereotypes to local editors, tracts, broadsides, pamphlets, and in one case a forged speech attributed to Alexander H. Stephens, whose alleged language was startlingly similar to that of Helper's *Impending Crisis*.

The word "propaganda" is an inexact expression which eludes definition. Every public appeal to support a cause could be loosely called propaganda. An advertisement might be propaganda in this broad sense, so also an editorial, a parade, a novel, a Sanitary Fair, a request for funds, a Thanksgiving proclamation, an anecdote, an envelope, a letter-head, a postage stamp, a dollar bill, a legislative preamble, a sermon, a petition, a sewing circle, or a school primer. One might use propaganda in christening a baby, naming a street, or addressing the Almighty. Motives in reaching the public were mixed. Propaganda in Lincoln's day was more often complex than simple, hybrid oftener than thoroughbred; it had one purpose grafted upon another. Publicity for the national cause was universal, but this broad appeal was often linked with an ulterior purpose which was in fact the main interest of the promoting agency. Thus a party rally would masquerade as a Union mass meeting, an appeal for peace in England might be an effort to withhold ironclads from the Confederacy, a volunteer fire brigade would be a unit of Tammany Hall, and the anniversary at Baltimore in 1862 of the anti-Union riot of April, 1861, was a boost for the newly elected mayor and council which had become Unionist. When Jay Cooke urged people to buy bonds he did not hesitate to blend self-interest with patriotism as he stressed the advantages of tax-free seven per cents. Even the name "Union" applied to the Republican party in Civil War days was an example of this tendency. Among themselves Republican leaders understood each other perfectly and continued to refer to their party as Republican, while for public consumption it was called "Union."

Much could be said of party propaganda, but this was not peculiar to war time; party agitation is always with us. That the national cause was appropriated for a party purpose was seen in the Union League. It is unnecessary to comment on the league at large, with its expensive club buildings, its social impressiveness, its exploitation of the American propensity for joining, its masses of war literature, and its showy efforts toward recruting and soldier relief; but there is need for further study of the league's campaign activities, especially the procedures of its local chap-

ters. The minute-book of a local league in the nineteenth ward of New York City belongs to the type of sources that are seldom dug up. The minutes here recorded are generally quite sterile as they creep along with routine matters till the approach of election time. Indeed it was not until September 19, 1864, that the nineteenth-ward leaguers "heartily approved" the early June nomination of Abraham Lincoln and Andrew Johnson at Baltimore. It was in October and the first days of November, 1864, that this local league suddenly came alive, sending loyal newspapers to soldiers, passing sizzling anti-Democratic resolutions, publishing campaign documents, and appointing poll-watchers to swing into action at sunrise on the eighth of November. Just after the election the minutes report "no quorum," and from that time this patriotic organization sank back into utter inactivity. Repeatedly there was the "no quorum" record; in February, 1865, it was voted to adopt measures to increase interest in the meetings. On April 3, 1865, the minutes flicker out altogether. Similar accounts with different terms, including the names of Tammany and the Knights of the Golden Circle, would illuminate the history of the Democratic party.

Official propaganda took many forms, including governmentally inspired foreign missions of prominent Americans. Thurlow Weed promoted the Union cause in the British press, Archbishop John Hughes sought contact with Catholics in Europe, Bishop McIlwaine of the Episcopal Church made his appeal to the British clergy. In addition, the irrepressible Robert J. Walker appealed to British financial groups in opposition to southern bond sales, while John M. Forbes and William H. Aspinwall labored to halt naval building for the Confederacy in Britain. President Lincoln, who once owned a newspaper, by no means neglected publicity. Naturally he addressed the people in occasional speeches, in his two inaugurals, his proclamations, and his messages to Congress. Beyond this there was the use of patronage for newspapers, an obscure subject yet to be explored, and there was the case of J. W. Forney whose Philadelphia *Chronicle* and Washington *Chronicle* were known as Lincoln organs. In March, 1862, the President asked Henry J. Raymond for an article in the *Times*. So much of the writing on Lincoln has been of the sentimentally stereotyped variety that people have overlooked Lincoln's trenchant comments on his own times, on wartime profits, on corruption, and on the manner in which every "foul bird" and "every dirty reptile" came forth in war time. It is safe to say that Lincoln saw the war more clearly and faced it more squarely than Emerson. He faced it with an amazing lack of hatred and rancor.

The Civil War generation, not alone military and political events, but life and *mores*, social conditions and thought-patterns that accompanied the war as well as non-war aspects of the age, will receive further attention by inquisitive historians. In Arthur C. Cole's pages in the Fox-Schlesinger series one finds many a cue for further investigation and many a product of mature study. Beyond the boundaries of even the newer books lie disappearing and forgotten stories. Where the stories are recoverable the present age of historiography, as shown in Cole's book, is more capable of accomplishing the recovery than previous ages. History has its vogues and its movements. Just as Americans beginning about 1935 executed something like an about-face in their interpretation of the World War, including American participation in it and attitudes preceding it, so the retelling of the Civil War is a matter of changed and changing viewpoints. In the present troubled age it may be of more than academic interest to reexamine the human beings of that war generation with less thought of the "splendor of battle flags" and with more of the sophisticated and unsentimental searchlight of reality.

Stressing the failure of the American political system, ROY F. NICHOLS (1896–), Professor Emeritus at the University of Pennsylvania has written a series of important works on the political history of the 1850s. In *The Disruption of American Democracy* he argues that the coming of the Civil War was the result of divisive attitudes of Democratic party factions and leaders. To what degree does the concluding chapter of his study, which follows, agree with Randall? Does Nichols offer a valid conclusion?*

Roy F. Nichols

Party Failure

The disruption of the American Democracy was complete in 1861. Secession had split the Republic, and the guns of civil war were thundering. The breakup of the Democratic party and the beginning of armed conflict were almost simultaneous; they were intimately related phenomena. The shattering of the party of Jackson was the bursting of a dike which unloosed an engulfing flood.

On the reasons for the Civil War there has been a vast amount of theorizing. Writers have been prone to select patterns—economic, cultural, political, racial, moral, and others—and to devise and emphasize theories in conformity with them. Long arguments as to whether the conflict was repressible or irrepressible, whether the war was inevitable or might have been avoided, have preoccupied historians. As they have unearthed more and more "causes," as they have introduced into the picture more and more elements, they have not altogether succeeded in answering the moot question: Why a civil war? Most of the principal "causes"—ideological differences, institutional differences, moral differences, cultural differences, sectional differences, physiographic differences—have existed in other times and places, without necessarily causing a war. Then why should they set the people of the United States to killing one another in 1861? . . .

People fight under the stress of hyperemotionalism. When some compelling

*Reprinted with permission of The Macmillan Company from *The Disruption of American Democracy* by Roy F. Nichols, pp. 513–517. Copyright 1948 by The Macmillan Company.

drive, whether it be ambition, fear, anger, or hunger, becomes supercharged, violence and bloodletting, thus far in human history, seem "inevitable." Now why was emotion in the United States in 1861 supercharged?

The basic reasons for this hyperemotionalism cannot be neatly formulated and weighted. Fundamentally the process was an illustration of what Machiavelli describes as the "confusion of a growing state." The population of the United States was rapidly multiplying, partly by natural increase and partly by foreign immigration, at the same time that it was arranging itself in rapidly changing patterns. Many Americans were creating new communities, others were crowding together into older urban centers. In old and new, change was continual, with a ceaseless moving out and coming in. The rate of growth, however, could not be uniform; for it was determined in large part by physiographical considerations and the Republic extended from the temperate into the semitropical zone. In the semitropical-to-temperate agricultural South, enterprise was less active, mobility less noticeable. In the northerly states, on the other hand, the variety of realized and potential wealth was greater, the stimulus from climate was sharper, the interest in projects of all sorts was more dynamic. There the vision of wealth and of the needs of the growing society continually inspired the creation of new and more powerful interests, under zealous and ambitious leaders.

So rapid and uneven a rate of social growth was bound to inflict upon Americans this "confusion of a growing state." Characteristic of it and dominant in it were pervasive, divisive, and cohesive attitudes which, as Whitman put it, were "significant of a grand upheaval of ideas and reconstruction of many things on new

bases." The social confusion in itself was the great problem confronting statesmen and politicians. Turn where they would, they could not escape it; they themselves were confused by it, and yet they must wrestle with it.

The political system which was in the process of evolving reflected their predicament. They knew that they were operating a federal system, but they oversimplified their problem by believing that it was only a political federalism. They did not grasp the fact that it was a cultural federalism as well. Not only were they dealing with a political federation of states, they must understand this cultural federation of attitudes. The inability to understand contributed much to their failure to organize partisanship and to create political machinery which would be adequate to deal with the complexities of this cultural federation.

This lack of understanding was accompanied by a deep-seated enjoyment of political activity by Americans which proved dangerous. They gave themselves so many opportunities to gratify their desire for this sport. There were so many elections and such constant agitation. Contests were scheduled automatically by the calendar, at many different times and seasons; there were thirty-three independent state systems of election. Within each state the parties, despite their national names, were really independent, each a law unto itself, and none was subjected to much if any central direction; there were nearly eighty such party organizations. A great disruptive fact was the baneful influence of elections almost continuously in progress, of campaigns never over, and of political uproar endlessly arousing emotions. The system of the fathers might possibly bear within itself the seeds of its own destruction.

This constant agitation certainly furnishes one of the primary clues to why the war came. It raised to ever higher pitch the passion-rousing oratory of rivals. They egged one another on to make more and more exaggerated statements to a people pervasively romantic and protestant, isolated and confused. The men and women exhibiting these different attitudes were not isolated and separated by boundaries—they dwelt side by side, and the same person might be moved by more than one attitude at a time, or by different attitudes at different times. The emotional complex which was created by the variety of these attitudes, and the tension which their antagonisms bred, added confusion to that already provided by the chaotic electoral customs and poorly organized parties; the total precipitated a resort to arms. The baffling problem was not how to maintain a balance among states but how to preserve a balance among a number of emotional units or attitudes. It was this that proved beyond the political capacity of the time.

The Democratic party was not unaware of some of the danger. Its most enlightened leaders had sought to quiet such divisive attitudes as antislaveryism in the North and southernism in the South by encouraging such cohesive attitudes as nationalism. Unhappily they did not understand the pervasive romanticism and protestantism sufficiently to make use of them in strengthening the cohesive attitudes. No leader in the Democracy could find the formula. Buchanan, Douglas, the justices of the Supreme Court, Davis, Hammond, and Hunter all tried and failed. The Republicans, such as Lincoln and Seward, grasped the realities: a house so divided against itself could not stand; with such divisive attitudes in the ascendant and unchecked, the conflict was irrepressible.

Under the stimulus of constant agita-

tion the leaders of the southern branch of the Democracy forbade the voters to elect a Republican President unless they wished him to preside over a shattered government. A number of voters sufficient to create a Republican majority in the Electoral College defied the prohibition. Then southerners, in a state of hyperemotion, moved by pride, self-interest, a sense of honor and fear, rushed to action; they were numerous enough and effective enough to force secession. They would flee the peril; in the spirit of 1776, they would organize a second American Revolution, this time against the tyranny not of a monarch but of "a mob." They would create a reformed confederacy free from corruption and centralization in which their social and economic institutions would be safe.

Also under the stimulus of constant agitation, the newly organized Republican administration decided to put down what it called the "Rebellion." Backed by an angered constituency including most northern Democrats, it determined to fight rather than permit the seceding states to break up a profitable partnership, a source of wealth and power, and an experiment in liberty and equality which Lincoln felt was the hope of the world. It undertook a "people's contest" to insure that "government of the people, by the people, for the people" should "not perish from the earth."

Thus war came when the American people for the first time refused to abide by a national election. The parties which had been promoting the cohesive attitudes had broken down, and their disorganization had permitted the new Republican organization to win through direct appeal to the divisive attitudes. The constant heat generated in the frequent elections brought an explosion. The social, economic, and cultural differences had been so used by the political operators as to produce secession and civil war.

War broke out because no means had been devised to curb the extravagant use of the divisive forces. Statesmanship seemed poverty-stricken. The work of the nationalists who sought to find a formula with which to overcome the divisive attitudes was vain. Too few even saw the need for the formula; they ran heedlessly down the path to disruption. The war was the product of the chaotic lack of system in ascertaining and directing the public will, a chaos exploited with little regard for the welfare of the general public by irresponsible and blind operators of local political machinery unchecked by any adequate central organization.

Finally, carrying the analysis even further, it may be postulated that the war came because of certain interests and activities characterized for convenience as the processes of human behavior, in which individual and general attitudes and emotional drives are constantly interacting — provoking and conditioning one another. At certain times and in certain circumstances, cooperative behavior predominates; but competitive behavior is seldom if ever absent, and when too vigorously aroused leads to a strife which ranges from argument to war. Indeed argument is itself a form of conflict short of war, more or less, and if pressed without checks and restraints easily passes over into war.

The American Democracy sought from 1850 to 1860 to keep in power by encouraging cooperative behavior. But, deeply affected by the shocks of the collisions occurring within the society in which it operated and of which it was a part, the party failed to overcome the divisive attitudes and was shattered. The disruption of the American Democracy eventuated in defeat, secession, and civil war.

ARTHUR SCHLESINGER, JR. (1917–   ) has written authoritative volumes on the age of Jackson, the age of Roosevelt, and the Kennedy era. A trusted adviser of President John F. Kennedy and of Senator Robert Kennedy, Schlesinger has been closely identified with the liberal attitudes of the New Frontier. Because of his personal involvement in public issues, his article on "The Causes of the American Civil War: A Note on Historical Sentimentalism," which appeared in the *Partisan Review* in 1949, has special significance. How does he refute the revisionists? In particular, how does he differ from Randall? Is his criticism valid? His approach also invites comparison with earlier assessments by James F. Rhodes.*

Arthur Schlesinger, Jr.

A Moral Problem

The Civil War was our great national trauma. A savage fraternal conflict, it released deep sentiments of guilt and remorse—sentiments which have reverberated through our history and our literature ever since. Literature in the end came to terms with these sentiments by yielding to the South in fantasy the victory it had been denied in fact; this tendency culminated on the popular level in *Gone with the Wind* and on the highbrow level in the Nashville cult of agrarianism. But history, a less malleable medium, was constricted by the intractable fact that the war had taken place, and by the related assumption that it was, in William H. Seward's phrase, an "irrepressible conflict," and hence a justified one.

As short a time ago as 1937, for example,

even Professor James G. Randall could describe himself as "unprepared to go to the point of denying that the great American tragedy could have been avoided." Yet in a few years the writing of history would succumb to the psychological imperatives which had produced *I'll Take my Stand* and *Gone with the Wind;* and Professor Randall would emerge as the leader of a triumphant new school of self-styled "revisionists." The publication of two vigorous books by Professor Avery Craven—*The Repressible Conflict* (1939) and *The Coming of the Civil War* (1942)—and the appearance of Professor Randall's own notable volumes on Lincoln—*Lincoln the President: Springfield to Gettysburg* (1945), *Lincoln and the South* (1946), and *Lincoln the Liberal Statesman*

---

*Arthur Schlesinger, Jr., "The Causes of the American Civil War: A Note on Historical Sentimentalism," *Partisan Review*, XVI, No. 10 (1949), pp. 969–981. Reprinted by permission from Professor Schlesinger.

(1947)—brought about a profound reversal of the professional historian's attitude toward the Civil War. Scholars now denied the traditional assumption of the inevitability of the war and boldly advanced the thesis that a "blundering generation" had transformed a "repressible conflict" into a "needless war."

The swift triumph of revisionism came about with very little resistance or even expressed reservations on the part of the profession. Indeed, the only adequate evaluation of the revisionist thesis that I know was made, not by an academic historian at all, but by that illustrious semi-pro, Mr. Bernard De Voto; and Mr. De Voto's two brilliant articles in *Harper's* in 1945 unfortunately had little influence within the guild. By 1947 Professor Allan Nevins, summing up the most recent scholarship in *Ordeal of the Union,* his able general history of the eighteen-fifties, could define the basic problem of the period in terms which indicated a measured but entire acceptance of revisionism. "The primary task of statesmanship in this era," Nevins wrote, "was to furnish a workable adjustment between the two sections, while offering strong inducements to the southern people to regard their labor system not as static but evolutionary, and equal persuasions to the northern people to assume a helpful rather than scolding attitude."

This new interpretation surely deserves at least as meticulous an examination as Professor Randall is prepared to give, for example, to such a question as whether or not Lincoln was playing fives when he received the news of his nomination in 1860. The following notes are presented in the interests of stimulating such an examination.

The revisionist case, as expounded by Professors Randall and Craven, has three main premises. First:

1) that the Civil War was caused by the irresponsible emotionalization of politics far out of proportion to the real problems involved. The war, as Randall put it, was certainly not caused by cultural variations nor by economic rivalries nor by sectional differences; these all existed, but it was "stupid," as he declared, to think that they required war as a solution. "One of the most colossal of misconceptions" was the "theory" that "fundamental motives produce war. The glaring and obvious fact is the artificiality of war-making agitation." After all, Randall pointed out, agrarian and industrial interests had been in conflict under Coolidge and Hoover; yet no war resulted. "In Illinois," he added, "major controversies (not mere transient differences) between downstate and metropolis have stopped short of war."

Nor was the slavery the cause. The issues arising over slavery were in Randall's judgment "highly artificial, almost fabricated. . . . They produced quarrels out of things that would have settled themselves were it not for political agitation." Slavery, Craven observed, was in any case a much overrated problem. It is "perfectly clear," he wrote, "that slavery played a rather minor part in the life of the South and of the Negro."

What then was the cause of war? "If one word or phrase were selected to account for the war," wrote Randall, ". . . it would have to be such a word as fanaticism (on both sides), misunderstanding, misrepresentation, or perhaps politics." Phrases like "whipped-up crisis" and "psychopathic case" adorned Randall's explanation. Craven similarly described the growing sense of sectional differences as "an artificial creation of inflamed minds." The "molders of public opinion steadily created the fiction of two distinct peoples." As a result, "distortion led a people into bloody war."

If uncontrolled emotionalism and fanaticism caused the war, how did they get out of hand? Who whipped up the "whipped-up crisis"? Thus the second revisionist thesis:

2) that sectional friction was permitted to develop into needless war by the inexcusable failure of political leadership in the fifties. "It is difficult to achieve a full realization of how Lincoln's generation stumbled into a ghastly war," wrote Randall. ". . . If one questions the term 'blundering generation,' let him inquire how many measures of the time he would wish copied or repeated if the period were to be approached with a clean slate and to be lived again."

It was the politicians, charged Craven, who systematically sacrificed peace to their pursuit of power. Calhoun and Adams, "seeking political advantage," mixed up slavery and expansion; Wilmot introduced his "trouble-making Proviso as part of the political game;" the repeal clause in the Kansas-Nebraska Act was "the afterthought of a mere handful of politicians;" Chase's Appeal to the Independent Democrats was "false in its assertions and unfair in its purposes, but it was politically effective"; the "damaging" section in the Dred Scott decision was forced "by the political ambitions of dissenting judges." "These uncalled-for moves and this irresponsible leadership," concluded Craven, blew up a "crack-pot" crusade into a national conflict.

It is hard to tell which was under attack here—the performance of a particular generation or democratic politics in general. But, if the indictment "blundering generation" meant no more than a general complaint that democratic politics placed a premium on emotionalism, then the Civil War would have been no more nor less "needless" than any event in our blundering history. The phrase "blundering generation" must consequently imply that the generation in power in the fifties was *below* the human or historical or democratic average in its blundering. Hence the third revisionist thesis:

3) that the slavery problem could have been solved without war. For, even if slavery were as unimportant as the revisionists have insisted, they would presumably admit that it constituted the real sticking-point in the relations between the sections. They must show therefore that there were policies with which a non-blundering generation could have resolved the slavery crisis and averted war; and that these policies were so obvious that the failure to adopt them indicated blundering and stupidity of a peculiarly irresponsible nature. If no such policies could be produced even by hindsight, then it would seem excessive to condemn the politicians of the fifties for failing to discover them at the time.

The revisionists have shown only a most vague and sporadic awareness of this problem. "Any kind of sane policy in Washington in 1860 might have saved the day for nationalism," remarked Craven; but he did not vouchsafe the details of these sane policies; we would be satisfied to know about one.* Similarly Randall declared that there were few policies of the fifties he would wish repeated if the period were to be lived over again; but he was not communicative about the policies he would wish pursued. Nevins likewise blamed the war on the "collapse of American statesmanship," but restrained himself from suggesting how a non-collapsible statesmanship would have solved the hard problems of the fifties.

---

*It is fair to say that Professor Craven seems in recent years to have modified his earlier extreme position; see his article "The Civil War and the Democratic Process," *Abraham Lincoln Quarterly*, June 1947.

In view of this reticence on a point so crucial to the revisionist argument, it is necessary to reconstruct the possibilities that might lie in the back of revisionism. Clearly there could be only two "solutions" to the slavery problem: the preservation of slavery, or its abolition.

Presumably the revisionists would not regard the preservation of slavery as a possible solution. Craven, it is true, has argued that "most of the incentives to honest and sustained effort, to a contented, well-rounded life, might be found under slavery. . . . What owning and being owned added to the normal relationship of employer and employee is very hard to say." In describing incidents in which slaves beat up masters, he has even noted that "happenings and reactions like these were the rule [sic], not the exception." But Craven would doubtless admit that, however jolly this system might have been, its perpetuation would have been, to say the least, impracticable.

If, then, revisionism has rested on the assumption that the nonviolent abolition of slavery was possible, such abolition could conceivably have come about through internal reform in the South; through economic exhaustion of the slavery system in the South; or through some government project for gradual and compensated emancipation. Let us examine these possibilities.

1) *The internal reform argument.* The South, the revisionists have suggested, might have ended the slavery system if left to its own devices; only the abolitionists spoiled everything by letting loose a hysteria which caused the southern ranks to close in self-defense.

This revisionist argument would have been more convincing if the decades of alleged anti-slavery feeling in the South had produced any concrete results. As one judicious southern historian, Professor Charles S. Sydnor, recently put it, "Although the abolition movement was followed by a decline of antislavery sentiment in the South, it must be remembered that in all the long years before that movement began no part of the South had made substantial progress toward ending slavery. . . . Southern liberalism had not ended slavery in any state."

In any case, it is difficult for historians seriously to suppose that northerners could have denied themselves feelings of disapproval over slavery. To say that there "should" have been no abolitionists in America before the Civil War is about as sensible as to say that there "should" have been no anti-Nazis in the nineteen-thirties or that there "should" be no anti-Communists today. People who indulge in criticism of remote evils may not be so pure of heart as they imagine; but that fact does not affect their inevitability as part of the historic situation.

Any theory, in short, which expects people to repress such spontaneous aversions is profoundly unhistorical. If revisionism has based itself on the conviction that things would have been different if only there had been no abolitionists, it has forgotten that abolitionism was as definite and irrevocable a factor in the historic situation as was slavery itself. And, just as abolitionism was inevitable, so too was the southern reaction against it—a reaction which, as Professor Clement Eaton has ably shown, steadily drove the free discussion of slavery out of the South. The extinction of free discussion meant, of course, the absolute extinction of any hope of abolition through internal reform.

2) *The economic exhaustion argument.* Slavery, it has been pointed out, was on the skids economically. It was overcapitalized and inefficient; it immobilized both capital and labor; its one-crop system

was draining the soil of fertility; it stood in the way of industrialization. As the South came to realize these facts, a revisionist might argue, it would have moved to abolish slavery for its own economic good. As Craven put it, slavery "may have been almost ready to break down of its own weight."

This argument assumed, of course, that southerners would have recognized the causes of their economic predicament and taken the appropriate measures. Yet such an assumption would be plainly contrary to history and to experience. From the beginning the South has always blamed its economic shortcomings, not on its own economic ruling class and its own inefficient use of resources, but on northern exploitation. Hard times in the eighteen-fifties produced in the South, not a reconsideration of the slavery system, but blasts against the North for the high prices of manufactured goods. The overcapitalization of slavery led, not to criticisms of the system, but to increasingly insistent demands for the reopening of the slave trade. Advanced southern writers like George Fitzhugh and James D. B. DeBow were even arguing that slavery was adapted to industrialism. When Hinton R. Helper did advance before the Civil War an early version of Craven's argument, asserting that emancipation was necessary to save the southern economy, the South burned his book. Nothing in the historical record suggests that the southern ruling class was preparing to deviate from its traditional pattern of self-exculpation long enough to take such a drastic step as the abolition of slavery.

3) *Compensated emancipation.* Abraham Lincoln made repeated proposals of compensated emancipation. In his annual message to Congress of December 1, 1862, he set forth a detailed plan by which States, on an agreement to abolish slavery

by 1900, would receive government bonds in proportion to the number of slaves emancipated. Yet, even though Lincoln's proposals represented a solution of the problem conceivably gratifying to the slaveholder's purse as well as to his pride, they got nowhere. Two-thirds of the border representatives rejected the scheme, even when personally presented to them by Lincoln himself. And, of course, only the pressure of war brought compensated emancipation its limited hearing of 1862.

Still, granted these difficulties, does it not remain true that other countries abolished slavery without internal convulsion? If emotionalism had not aggravated the situation beyond hope, Craven has written, then slavery "might have been faced as a national question and dealt with as successfully as the South American countries dealt with the same problem." If Brazil could free its slaves and Russia its serfs in the middle of the nineteenth century without civil war, why could not the United States have done as well?

The analogies are appealing but not, I think, really persuasive. There are essential differences between the slavery question in the United States and the problems in Brazil or in Russia. In the first place, Brazil and Russia were able to face servitude "as a national question" because it was, in fact, a national question. Neither country had the American problem of the identification of compact sectional interests with the survival of the slavery system. In the second place, there was no race problem at all in Russia; and, though there was a race problem in Brazil, the more civilized folkways of that country relieved racial differences of the extreme tension which they breed in the South of the United States. In the third place, neither in Russia nor in Brazil did the abolition of servitude involve constitutional issues; and the existence of these issues played a great part in determining the form of the American struggle.

It is hard to draw much comfort, therefore, from the fact that other nations abolished servitude peaceably. The problem in America was peculiarly recalcitrant. The schemes for gradual emancipation got nowhere. Neither internal reform nor economic exhaustion contained much promise for a peaceful solution. The hard fact, indeed, is that the revisionists have not tried seriously to describe the policies by which the slavery problem could have been peacefully resolved. They have resorted instead to broad affirmations of faith: if only the conflict could have been staved off long enough, then somehow, somewhere, we could have worked something out. It is legitimate, I think, to ask how? where? what?—at least, if these affirmations of faith are to be used as the premise for castigating the unhappy men who had the practical responsibility for finding solutions and failed.

Where have the revisionists gone astray? In part, the popularity of revisionism obviously parallels that of *Gone with the Wind*—the victors paying for victory by pretending literary defeat. But the essential problem is why history should be so vulnerable to this literary fashion; and this problem, I believe, raises basic questions about the whole modern view of history. It is perhaps stating the issue in too portentous terms. Yet I cannot escape the feeling that the vogue of revisionism is connected with the modern tendency to seek in optimistic sentimentalism an escape from the severe demands of moral decision; that it is the offspring of our modern sentimentality which at once evades the essential moral problems in the name of a superficial objectivity and asserts their unimportance in the name of an invincible progress.

The revisionists first glided over the implications of the fact that the slavery system was producing a closed society in the South. Yet that society increasingly had justified itself by a political and philosophical repudiation of free society; southern thinkers swiftly developed the anti-liberation potentialities in a social system whose cornerstone, in Alexander H. Stephen's proud phrase, was human bondage. In theory and in practice, the South organized itself with mounting rigor against ideas of human dignity and freedom, because such ideas inevitably threatened the basis of their own system. Professor Frank L. Owsley, the southern agrarian, has described inadvertently but accurately the direction in which the slave South was moving. "The abolitionists and their political allies were threatening the existence of the South as seriously as the Nazis threaten the existence of England," wrote Owsley in 1940; ". . . Under such circumstances the surprising thing is that so little was done by the South to defend its existence."

There can be no question that many southerners in the fifties had similar sentiments; that they regarded their system of control as ridiculously inadequate; and that, with the book-burning, the censorship of the mails, the gradual illegalization of dissent, the South was in process of creating a real machinery of repression in order more effectively "to defend its existence." No society, I suppose, encourages criticism of its basic institutions. Yet, when a democratic society acts in self-defense, it does so at least in the name of human dignity and freedom. When a society based on bond slavery acts to eliminate criticism of its peculiar institution, it outlaws what a believer in democracy can only regard as the abiding values of man. When the basic institutions are evil, in other words, the effect of attempts to defend their existence can only be the moral and intellectual stultification of the society.

A society closed in the defense of evil institutions thus creates moral differences far too profound to be solved by compromise. Such a society forces upon every one, both those living at the time and those writing about it later, the necessity for a moral judgment; and the moral judgment in such cases becomes an indispensable factor in the historical understanding.

The revisionists were commendably anxious to avoid the vulgar errors of the post-Civil War historians who pronounced smug individual judgments on the persons involuntarily involved in the tragedy of the slave system. Consequently they tried hard to pronounce no moral judgments at all on slavery. Slavery became important, in Craven's phrase, "only as a very ancient labor system, probably at this time rather near the end of its existence"; the attempt to charge this labor system with moral meanings was "a creation of inflamed imaginations." Randall, talking of the Kansas-Nebraska Act, could describe it as "a law intended to subordinate the slavery question and hold it in *proper* proportion" (my italics). I have quoted Randall's even more astonishing argument that, because major controversies between downstate and metropolis in Illinois stopped short of war, there was reason to believe that the Civil War could have been avoided. Are we to take it that the revisionists seriously believe that the downstate-metropolis fight in Illinois — or the agrarian-industrial fight in the Coolidge and Hoover administrations — were in any useful sense comparable to the difference between the North and South in 1861?

Because the revisionists felt no moral urgency themselves, they deplored as fanatics those who did feel it, or brushed aside their feelings as the artificial product of emotion and propaganda. The revisionist hero was Stephen A. Douglas, who always thought that the great moral problems could be solved by sleight-of-hand. The phrase "northern man of southern sentiments," Randall remarked, was "said opprobriously . . . as if it were a base thing for a northern man to work with his southern fellows."

By denying themselves insight into the moral dimension of the slavery crisis, in other words, the revisionists denied themselves a historical understanding of the intensities that caused the crisis. It was the moral issue of slavery, for example, that gave the struggles over slavery in the territories or over the enforcement of the fugitive slave laws their significance. These issues, as the revisionists have shown with cogency, were not in themselves basic. But they were the available issues; they were almost the only points within the existing constitutional framework where the moral conflict could be faced; as a consequence, they became charged with the moral and political dynamism of the central issue. To say that the Civil War was fought over the "unreal" issue of slavery in the territories is like saying that the Second World War was fought over the "unreal" issue of the invasion of Poland. The democracies could not challenge fascism inside Germany any more than opponents of slavery could challenge slavery inside the South; but the extension of slavery, like the extension of fascism, was an act of aggression which made a moral choice inescapable.

Let us be clear what the relationship of moral judgment to history is. Every historian, as we all know in an argument that surely does not have to be repeated in 1949, imports his own set of moral judgments into the writing of history by the very process of interpretation; and the phrase "every historian" includes the category "revisionist." Mr. De Voto in his paraphrases of the revisionist position has put admirably the contradictions on this point: as for "moral questions, God forbid. History will not put itself in the position of saying that any thesis may have been wrong, any cause evil. . . . History will not deal with moral values, though of course the Republican radicals were, well, culpable." The whole revisionist attitude toward abolitionists and radicals, repeatedly characterized by Randall as "unctuous" and "intolerant," overflows with the moral feeling which is so virtuously excluded from discussions of slavery.

An acceptance of the fact of moral responsibility does not license the historian to roam through the past ladling out individual praise and blame: such an attitude would ignore the fact that all individuals, including historians, are trapped in a web of circumstance which curtails their moral possibilities. But it does mean that there are certain essential issues on which it is necessary for the historian to have a position if he is to understand the great conflicts of history. These great conflicts are relatively few because there are few enough historical phenomena which we can confidently identify as evil. The essential issues appear, moreover, not in pure and absolute form, but incomplete and imperfect, compromised by the deep complexity of history. Their proponents may often be neurotics and fanatics, like the abolitionists. They may attain a social importance only when a configuration of non-moral factors—economic, political, social, military—permit them to do so.

Yet neither the nature of the context nor the pretensions of the proponents alter the character of the issue. And human slavery is certainly one of the few issues of whose evil we can be sure. It is not just "a very ancient labor system"; it is also a betrayal of the basic values of our Christian and democratic tradition. No historian can understand the circumstances which led to its abolition until he writes about it in its fundamental moral context. "History is supposed to understand the difference between a decaying economy and an expanding one," as Mr. De Voto well said, "between solvency and bankruptcy, between a dying social idea and one coming to world acceptance. . . . It is even supposed to understand implications of the difference between a man who is legally a slave and one who is legally free."

"Revisionism in general has no position," De Voto continues, "but only a vague sentiment." Professor Randall well suggested the uncritical optimism of that sentiment when he remarked, "To suppose that the Union could not have been continued or slavery outmoded without the war and without the corrupt concomitants of war is hardly an enlightened assumption." We have here a touching afterglow of the admirable nineteenth-century faith in the full rationality and perfectibility of man; the faith that the errors of the world would all in time be "outmoded" (Professor Randall's use of this word is suggestive) by progress. Yet the experience of the twentieth century has made it clear that we gravely overrated man's capacity to solve the problems of existence within the terms of history.

This conclusion about man may disturb our complacencies about human nature. Yet it is certainly more in accord with history than Professor Randall's "enlightened" assumption that man can solve peacefully all the problems which overwhelm him. The unhappy fact is that man occasionally works himself into a log-jam; and that the log-jam must be burst by violence. We know that well enough from the experience of the last decade. Are we to suppose that some future historian will echo Professor Nevins' version of the "failure" of the eighteen-fifties and write: "The primary task of statesmanship in the nineteen-thirties was to furnish a workable adjustment between the United States and Germany, while offering strong inducements to the German people to abandon the police state and equal persuasions to the Americans to help the Nazis rather than scold them?" Will some future historian adapt Professor Randall's formula and write that the word "appeaser" was used "opprobriously" as if it were a "base" thing for an American to work with his Nazi fellow? Obviously this revisionism of the future (already foreshadowed in the work of Charles A. Beard) would represent, as we now see it, a fantastic evasion of the hard and unpleasant problems of the thirties. I doubt whether our present revisionism would make much more sense to the men of the eighteen-fifties.

The problem of the inevitability of the Civil War, of course, is in its essence a problem devoid of meaning. The revisionist attempt to argue that the war could have been avoided by "any kind of sane policy" is of interest less in its own right than as an expression of a characteristically sentimental conception of man and of history. And the great vogue of revisionism in the historical profession suggests, in my judgment, ominous weaknesses in the contemporary attitude toward history.

We delude ourselves when we think that history teaches us that evil will be "outmoded" by progress and that politics consequently does not impose on us the necessity for decision and for struggle. If historians are to understand the fullness of the social dilemma they seek to reconstruct, they must understand that sometimes there is no escape from the implacabilities of moral decision. When social conflicts embody great moral issues, these conflicts cannot be assigned for solution to the invincible march of progress; nor can they be bypassed with "objective" neutrality. Not many problems perhaps force this decision upon the historian. But, if any problem does in our history, it is the Civil War.

To reject the moral actuality of the Civil War is to foreclose the possibility of an adequate account of its causes. More than that, it is to misconceive and grotesquely to sentimentalize the nature of history. For history is not a redeemer, promising to solve all human problems in time; nor is man capable of transcending the limitations of his being. Man generally is entangled in insoluble problems; history is consequently a tragedy in which we are all involved, whose keynote is anxiety and frustration, not progress and fulfillment. Nothing exists in history to assure us that the great moral dilemmas can be resolved without pain; we cannot therefore be relieved from the duty of moral judgment on issues so appalling and inescapable as those involved in human slavery; nor can we be consoled by sentimental theories about the needlessness of the Civil War into regarding our own struggles against evil as equally needless.

One must emphasize, however, that this duty of judgment applies to issues. Because we are all implicated in the same tragedy, we must judge the men of the past with the same forbearance and charity which we hope the future will apply toward us.

CHARLES W. RAMSDELL (1877–1942) was perhaps the most eloquent spokesman for the Southern interpretation of the immediate causes of the Civil War. A loyal son of his section, Ramsdell, who taught for many years at the University of Texas, attempted to prove that Lincoln deliberately provoked the Confederacy into firing the first shot at Fort Sumter. The article which follows represents the summary of his findings.*

Charles W. Ramsdell

Fort Sumter a Deliberate Plot

When the Confederate batteries around Charleston Harbor opened fire on Fort Sumter in the early morning hours of April 12, 1861, they signaled the beginning of the most calamitous tragedy in the history of the American people. Because the Confederate authorities ordered the attack it is generally held that they were directly responsible for the horrors of the ensuing four years. Certainly that was the feeling in the North, then and afterwards, and it became the verdict of austere historians.

Whether the war was inevitable, in any case, is a question that need not be raised here. It has been the subject of endless disputation and is one to which no conclusive answer can be given. But even though it be conceded that if the conflict had not arisen from the Fort Sumter crisis it would have sprung from some other incident growing out of the secession of the "cotton states," the actual firing of the "first shot" placed the Southerners under a great moral and material disadvantage. The general Northern conviction that the "rebels" had made an unprovoked attack upon the little Federal garrison added thousands of volunteers to the Union armies and strengthened the determination of the Northern people to carry the struggle through to the complete subjugation of the South.

The Confederate leaders who ordered the bombardment were not vicious, feeble-minded, irresponsible, or inexperi-

*Charles W. Ramsdell, "Lincoln and Fort Sumter," *Journal of Southern History,* III (1937), 259–288. (Footnotes omitted). Copyright 1937 by the Southern Historical Association. Reprinted by permission of the Managing Editor.

enced men. As even a casual investigation will show, they had been fully aware of the danger of taking the initiative in hostilities and had hoped for peace. How then could they be so blind as to place themselves at this manifest disadvantage?

The story of the development of the Fort Sumter crisis has been told many times, but it is so full of complexities that there is little wonder that many of its most significant features have been obscured with a resultant loss of perspective. On the one hand, most accounts have begun with certain assumptions which have affected the interpretation of the whole mass of evidence; on the other, too little credit has been given to Abraham Lincoln's genius for political strategy, which is truly surprising in view of all the claims that have been made for the abilities of that very remarkable man. The purpose of this paper is to place the facts already known in their logical and chronological order and to re-evalutate them in that setting in the belief that when thus arranged they will throw new light upon this momentous affair.

The early stages of the Sumter problem can be dealt with in summary form. It is well known that six days after the secession of South Carolina Major Robert Anderson, who had been stationed at Fort Moultrie in command of all the United States forces in Charleston Harbor, abandoned Moultrie and moved his command into the new and still unfinished Fort Sumter where he thought his force would be better able to resist attack. The South Carolina authorities evidently had had no intention of attacking him for they thought they had an understanding with President Buchanan for maintaining the military status quo; but they immediately occupied Fort Moultrie and Castle Pinckney and made protest to Buchanan, demanding that Anderson be sent back to

Moultrie. Buchanan refused to admit their ground of protest or to order Anderson back; then early in January he ordered relief to be sent secretly to the garrison on a merchant steamer. This vessel, *The Star of the West,* was forced back from the entrance of the harbor by the military authorities of the state, and the South Carolinians were with some difficulty restrained by the leaders in other Southern states from assaulting Fort Sumter. Thereafter Buchanan refrained from the use of force, partly because Anderson insisted that he was in no danger, partly because he still hoped for some peaceful adjustment, if not by Congress itself, then by the Peace Conference which was soon to assemble in Washington, and partly because he was averse during the last weeks of his term to beginning hostilities for which he was unprepared.

By February 1 six other cotton states had passed ordinances of secession and each of them, as a matter of precaution and largely because of the happenings at Charleston, seized the forts, arsenals, customs houses, and navy yards within its own borders. There were two exceptions, both in Florida. Fort Taylor, at Key West, was left undisturbed; and Fort Pickens, at the entrance of Pensacola Bay and on the extreme western tip of Santa Rosa Island, was occupied by a small Federal force much as Fort Sumter had been.

Since Fort Pickens plays a part in the development of the Sumter crisis, some explanation of the situation at that point becomes necessary. In the beginning this fort was not occupied by troops, but a company of artillery, under Lieutenant Adam J. Slemmer, was stationed at Barrancas Barracks, across the neck of the bay about a mile and a half to the north of Pickens, and close by the Navy Yard. The town of Pensacola was some six miles farther up the bay. On January 10 Lieutenant Slemmer, hearing that the governors of Florida and Alabama were about to send troops to seize the forts and the Navy Yard and in accordance with instructions from General Winfield Scott, removed his small command to Fort Pickens. On the twelfth the Navy Yard capitulated to the combined state forces under Colonel W. H. Chase. Chase then demanded the surrender of Fort Pickens, which Slemmer refused. After some further correspondence between the two opposing officers, a group of nine Southern senators in Washington, on January 18, urged that no attack should be made on Fort Pickens because it was "not worth a drop of blood." These senators believed that the Republicans in Congress were hoping to involve the Buchanan administration in hostilities in order that war might open before Lincoln's inauguration. On January 29 an agreement was effected at Washington by Senator Stephen R. Mallory of Florida, and others, with President Buchanan and his secretaries of War and the Navy to the effect that no reinforcement would be sent to Fort Pickens and no attack would be made upon it by the secessionists. The situation at Fort Pickens then became somewhat like that at Fort Sumter; but there were certain differences. Fort Pickens did not threaten the town of Pensacola as Fort Sumter did Charleston; it was easily accessible from the sea if reinforcements should be decided upon; and there was no such excitement over its continued occupation by United States troops as there was about Sumter.

As soon as the new Confederate government was organized the Confederate Congress, on February 12, by resolution took charge of "questions existing between the several States of this Confederacy and the United States respecting the occupation of forts, arsenals, navy yards and other pub-

lic establishments." This hurried action was taken in order to get the management of the Sumter question out of the hands of the impatient and rather headlong Governor Francis W. Pickens of South Carolina, who, it was feared, might precipitate war at any time. In fact, the public mind, North and South, sensed accurately that the greatest danger to peace lay in Charleston Harbor.

This danger, of course, was in the irreconcilable views of the two governments concerning their respective claims to the fort. To the Washington officials Sumter was not merely the legal property of the Federal government; its possession was a symbol of the continuity and integrity of that government. To withdraw the garrison at the demand of the secessionists would be equivalent to acknowledging the legality of secession and the dissolution of the Union. There was also, especially with the military officials, a point of honor involved; they could not yield to threats of force. The attitude of the Southerners was based upon equally imperative considerations. In their view the Confederate States no longer had any connection with the government on the Potomac; they were as independent as that other seceded nation, Belgium. No independent government could maintain its own self-respect or the respect of foreign governments if it permitted another to hold an armed fortress within the harbor of one of its principal cities. When South Carolina had ceded the site for the fortification it had done so for its own protection. That protection was now converted into a threat, for the guns of Sumter dominated not only every point in the harbor but the city of Charleston itself. We may conceive an analogous situation by supposing that Great Britain at the close of the American Revolution had insisted upon retaining a fortress within the harbor of Boston or of New York. The Confederate government could not, without yielding the principle of independence, abate its claims to the fort.

During the last six weeks of Buchanan's term the situation at Charleston remained relatively quiet. Anderson and his engineers did what they could to strengthen the defenses of Sumter; while the state and Confederate officers established batteries around the harbor both to repel any future relief expedition and, in case of open hostilities, to reduce the fort. Although Governor Pickens had wished to press demands for surrender and to attack the fort if refused, he had first sought the advice of such men as Governor Joseph E. Brown of Georgia and Jefferson Davis of Mississippi. Both advised against any such action, partly because they still had some hope of peace and partly because they saw the danger of taking the initiative. Although Anderson was under constant surveillance, he was allowed free use of the mails and was permitted to purchase for his men fresh meats and vegetables in the Charleston market. Other necessities, which under army regulations he must procure from the regular supply departments of the army, he was not allowed to receive because that would be permitting the Federal government to send relief to the garrison and involve an admission of its right to retain the fort. Anderson consistently informed the authorities at Washington during this time that he was safe and that he could hold out indefinitely. The Confederate government, having taken over from the state all negotiations concerning the fort, was moving cautiously with the evident hope of avoiding hostilities. On February 15 the Confederate Congress by resolution requested President Davis to appoint three commissioners to negotiate with the United States "all questions of disagreement between the two governments" and Davis appointed them on February 25. They reached Washington on March 5, the day after Lincoln's inauguration.

Southern as well as Northern men waited anxiously to learn what policy would be indicated by the new President of the United States in his inaugural address. It is not necessary to dwell long on what Abraham Lincoln said in that famous paper. He stated plainly that he regarded the Union as unbroken, the secession of the seven cotton states as a nullity. In this he merely took the position that Buchanan had taken. He also said that he would enforce the laws of the Union in all the states; but he immediately softened this declaration by saying that he would not use violence unless it should be forced upon the national authority. Then he added, "The power confided to me will be used to hold, occupy and possess the property and places belonging to the government, and to collect the duties and imposts; but beyond what may be necessary for these objects, there will be no invasion, no using of force against or among the people anywhere." And later on: "In your hands, my dissatisfied fellow countrymen, and not in mine, is the momentous issue of civil war. The government will not assail you. You can have no conflict without being yourselves the aggressors." How is it possible to reconcile the declaration that he would occupy "the property and places belonging to the government" with the promise that the government would not assail his dissatisfied fellow countrymen who either held or claimed the right to those places? While ostensibly addressing the Southerners, was he really directing these last soothing words to the anxious antiwar elements in the North? Although it is improbable that he had this early any definite plan in mind, his warning that the secessionists would be the aggressors, if civil war should come, may be significant in view of what he was to be engaged in exactly a month from that day.

But the inaugural should not be regarded as the declaration of a definite program; for while the new President was careful to lay down the general principle that the Union was legally unbroken, he refrained with equal care from committing himself to any course of action. If he hedged at every point where a statement of active policy was expected, it was because he could not know what he would be able to do. Caution was necessary; it was not merely political expediency, it was at that juncture political wisdom. Cautious reticence, until he knew his way was clear, was a very marked trait of Abraham Lincoln. There is another characteristic quality in this address. Lincoln had developed an extraordinary skill in so phrasing his public utterances as to arouse in each special group he singled out for attention just the reaction he desired. To the extreme and agressive Republicans the inaugural indicated a firm determination to enforce obedience upon the secessionists; to the Northern moderates and peace advocates, as well as to the anxious Unionists of the border slave states, not yet seceded, it promised a conciliatory attitude; in the seceded states it was interpreted as threatening coercion and had the effect of hastening preparations for defense.

In the latter part of the address Lincoln had counseled the people generally to avoid precipitate action and to take time to think calmly about the situation. He doubtless hoped to be able to take time himself; but he discovered within a few hours that there was one problem whose solution could not be long postponed. On the very day of his inauguration Buchanan's secretary of war, Joseph Holt, received a letter from Major Anderson in which for the first time the commander at

Fort Sumter expressed doubt of his ability to maintain himself. More than this, Anderson estimated that, in the face of the Confederate batteries erected about the harbor, it would require a powerful fleet and a force of twenty thousand men to give permanent relief to the garrison. Since it was his last day in office, Buchanan had the letter referred to Lincoln; and when on March 5 Holt submitted it to the new President he accompanied it with a report sharply reviewing Anderson's previous assurances of his safety. Lincoln called General Scott into conference and the General concurred with Anderson. After a few days of further consideration Scott was of the same opinion and was sustained by General Joseph G. Totten, chief of the Army Engineers. These men considered the question primarily as a military problem, although Scott could not refrain from injecting political considerations into his written statement. In doing this the aged General was suspected of following the lead of Secretary William H. Seward who was already urging the evacuation of Sumter, in order to avoid precipitating hostilities at that point, and the reinforcement of Fort Pickens in order to assert the authority of the government. Lincoln accepted at least a part of Seward's plan, for on March 12, General Scott, by the President's direction, sent an order to Captain Israel Vogdes, whose artillery company was on board the U.S. Steamer *Brooklyn,* lying off Fort Pickens, directing him to land his company, reinforce Pickens, and hold it. Instead of sending the order overland, Scott sent it around by sea with the result that it did not reach its destination until April 1, and then the navy captain in command of the ship on which the artillery company was quartered refused to land the troops because the orders from the former Secretary of the Navy directing him to respect the truce with the Confederates had never been countermanded. The fort was not reinforced at that time, a fact of which Lincoln remained ignorant until April 6. We shall return to the Fort Pickens situation later.

Meanwhile Lincoln was considering the Fort Sumter problem. He had learned that Anderson's supplies were running short and that the garrison could not hold out much longer without relief. Although both General Scott and General Totten had advised that the relief of the fort was impracticable with the forces available, Gustavus V. Fox, a former officer of the navy and a brother-in-law of Postmaster-General Montgomery Blair, believed that it would be possible to reach the fort by running small steamers past the Confederate batteries at the entrance to the harbor. Fox had first proposed this to Scott early in February; he now came forward again with the backing of Montgomery Blair and presented his plan and arguments to Lincoln on March 13. The President seems to have been impressed, for on March 15 he asked for the written opinions of his cabinet on the question whether, assuming that it was now possible to provision Sumter, it was wise to attempt it. All, save Montgomery Blair, advised against an expedition. Apparently this overwhelming majority of his cabinet at first decided him against the plans, for there is considerable evidence, although it is not conclusive, that he was about to order Anderson to evacuate. Certainly rumors of impending orders for evacuation were coming from various high official circles in Washington aside from those for which Seward seems to have been responsible. There is the familiar story of how old Frank Blair, brought to the White House by his son Montgomery, found the President about to sign the evacuation order and protested so vigorously that Lincoln did not sign it.

Lincoln now found himself facing a most difficult and dangerous situation and the more he considered it the more troublesome it appeared. It seems reasonably certain that he never wanted to give up Sumter. As early as December 24, 1860, having heard a wild rumor that the forts in South Carolina were to be surrendered by the order or consent of President Buchanan, he had written from Springfield to Senator Lyman Trumbull that he would, "if our friends at Washington concur, announce publicly at once that they are to be retaken after the inauguration." After he had arrived at Washington and had taken up the burden of office he saw that the problem was not so simple as it had looked from the frontier town of Springfield. His Secretary of State, a man of far greater political experience than himself, was urging him to make his stand for the authority of the government at Fort Pickens and not at Sumter, for Seward could not see how it would be possible to reinforce Sumter without putting the administration in the position of the aggressor. That would be a fatal mistake. Fort Pickens, on the other hand, could be relieved from the Gulf side without coming into direct conflict with the Confederates.

It would be extremely interesting to know what was passing through Lincoln's mind during those difficult days when, bedeviled by importunate office seekers, he could find little time for considering what he should do about the re-establishment of Federal authority in the seceded states and especially about the imperiled fort at Charleston. As was his habit, he left few clues to his reflections and it is impossible to say with assurance what ideas he picked up, examined, and discarded. One plan which he seems to have entertained for a short while, just after the adverse cabinet vote on relieving Sumter, contemplated the collection of customs duties on revenue vessels, supported by ships of war, just outside the Confederate ports; and there were hints in the press that Anderson's force was to be withdrawn to a ship off Charleston. If it were seriously considered, the plan was soon abandoned, possibly because of legal impediments or more probably because it did not fully meet the needs of the situation. But although Lincoln kept his thoughts to himself he must have studied public opinion closely, and we may be able to follow his thinking if we examine for ourselves the attitudes of the several groups in the North as they revealed themselves in those uncertain days of March.

It must not be forgotten that, notwithstanding Lincoln's smashing victory in the free states in November, his party was still new and relatively undisciplined. His support had come from a heterogeneous mass of voters and for a variety of reasons. The slavery issue, the drive for a protective tariff and internal improvements, the promise of free homesteads in the West, and disgust at the split among the Democrats had each played its part. Many voters had been persuaded that there was no real danger of a disruption of the Union in the event of his election. The secession of the border states had now thrown the former issues into the background and thrust to the front the question whether the discontented Southerners should be allowed to depart in peace or whether the government should, as Lincoln phrased it, "enforce the laws" and in so doing bring on war with the newly formed Confederacy. As always, when a new and perilous situation arises, the crosscurrents of public opinion were confusing. As Lincoln, pressed on all sides, waited while he studied the drift, he could not fail to note that there was a strong peace party in the North which was urging the settlement of difficulties without resort to force. On the other hand the

more aggressive party men among the Republicans, to whom he was under special obligations, were insisting that he exert the full authority of the government even to the extent of war. This group included some of the most active and powerful members of his party whom he could not afford to antagonize. One disturbing factor in the situation was the marked tendency of many voters who had supported him in November to turn against the Republicans, as was shown in a number of local elections in Ohio and New England. While the peace men attributed this reversal to fear of war, the more aggressive Republicans insisted that it was caused by disgust at the rumors that Fort Sumter would be given up to the secessionists. Reinforcing the Northern conservatives were the majorities in the eight border slave states who had thus far refused to secede but who were openly opposed to any "coercive" action against their brethren in the Lower South. The Virginia State Convention, which had convened on February 13 and was in complete control of the conditional Unionists, was still in session, evidently awaiting his decision. Therefore, if he should adopt a strongly aggressive policy he might find himself opposed by the large group of peace men in the North while he precipitated most if not all of the border slave states into secession and union with the Confederacy. If, on the other hand, he failed to act decisively, he was very likely to alienate the radical Republicans who were already manifesting impatience. In either case he would divide his party at the very beginning of his administration and increase the risk of utter failure. There was, however, some cheering evidence among the business elements of a growing irritation against the secessionists because of the depression which had set in with the withdrawal of South Carolina; and if the Confederates should add further offense to their low tarriff policy or adopt more aggressive tactics with respect to the forts, this feeling might grow strong enough to overcome the peace men.

He had promised to maintain the Union, but how was he to attempt it without wrecking his chances at the very outset? It was now too late to restore the Union by compromise because, having himself rejected all overtures in December, he could not now afford to offer what he had recently refused. Moreover, there was no indication that the Confederates would accept at this late date any compromise he might proffer. He must do something, for the gradual exhaustion of the supplies of the garrison in Fort Sumter would soon force his hand. He could not order Anderson to evacuate without arousing the wrath of the militant Unionists in the North. If he continued to let matters drift, Anderson himself would have to evacuate when his supplies were gone. While that would relieve the administration of any charge of coercion, it would expose the government to the accusation of disgraceful weakness and improve the chances of the Confederacy for foreign recognition. If he left Anderson to his fate and made ostentatious display of reinforcing Fort Pickens, as Seward was urging him to do, would he gain as much as he lost? Was it not best, even necessary, to make his stand at Sumter? But if he should try to relieve Anderson by force of arms, what was the chance of success? Anderson, supported by the high authority of General Scott, thought there was none. If, as Captain Fox believed, swift steamers could run the gauntlet of the Confederate batteries and reach the fort with men and supplies, would they then be able to hold it against attack? Failure in this military movement might seriously damage the already uncertain prestige of the administration. Would it not be looked upon as aggressive war by the border state men and perhaps by the peace men in the North? Could he risk the handicap of appearing to force civil war upon the country? In every direction the way out of his dilemma seemed closed.

There was one remote possibility: the Confederates themselves might precipitate matters by attacking Sumter before Anderson should be compelled to evacuate by lack of supplies. But the Confederates, though watchful, were showing great caution. General P. G. T. Beauregard, in command at Charleston since March 6, was treating Major Anderson with elaborate courtesy. The government at Montgomery was in no hurry to force the issue, partly because it was quite well aware of the danger of assuming the aggressive and partly because it was waiting to see what its commissioners would be able to effect at Washington, where Seward was holding out hopes to them of the eventual evacuation of Sumter. At some time, while turning these things over in his mind, this daring thought must have occurred to Lincoln: Could the Southerners be *induced* to attack Sumter, to assume the aggressive and thus put themselves in the wrong in the eyes of the North and of the world? If they could, the latent irritation perceptible among the Northern moderates might flame out against the secessionists and in support of the government. The two wings of his party would unite, some at least of the Democrats would come to his support, even the border-state people might be held, if they could be convinced that the war was being forced by the secessionists. Unless he could unite them in defense of the authority of the government, the peaceable and the "stiff-backed" Republicans would split apart, the party would collapse, his administration would be a failure, and he would go down in history as a weak man who had allowed the Union to crumble in his hands. As things now stood, the only way by which the Union could be restored, his party and his administration saved, was by an unequivocal assertion of the authority of the government, that is, through war. But he must not openly assume the aggressive; that must be done by the secessionists. The best opportunity was at Fort Sumter, but the time left was short for Anderson was running short of essential supplies.

Let us examine closely what Lincoln did after the middle of March, taking care to place each movement as nearly as possible in its exact sequence. We have seen that Captain Fox made his argument to Lincoln for a combined naval and military expedition on March 13 and that the cabinet, with the exception of Montgomery Blair and the equivocal Chase, had voted against it on the fifteenth. Fox then offered to go in person to Fort Sumter to investigate the situation and Lincoln gave him permission. He arrived in Charleston on March 21 and was allowed to see Anderson that night. He and Anderson agreed that the garrison could not hold out longer than noon of April 15. Although Anderson seems to have remained unconvinced of its feasibility, Fox returned to Washington full of enthusiasm for his plan.

On the very day that Fox arrived in Charleston, Lincoln had dispatched to that city a close friend and loyal supporter, Ward H. Lamon, a native of Virginia and his former law partner in Illinois. This sending of Lamon on the heels of Fox is an interesting incident. The precise nature of his instructions has never been fully revealed. Lamon himself, in his *Recollections,* merely says he was sent "on a confidential mission" and intimates that he was to report on the extent

of Unionist feeling in South Carolina. He arrived in Charleston on the night of Saturday, March 23; visited James L. Petigru, the famous Unionist, on Sunday and learned from him that there was no Unionist strength in the state, that "peaceable secession or war was inevitable"; and on Monday morning obtained an interview with Governor Pickens. In reply to questions the Governor stated very positively that any attempt on the part of President Lincoln to reinforce Sumter would bring on war, that only his "unalterable resolve *not* to attempt any reinforcement" could prevent war. Lamon, whether through innocence or guile, left the impression with the Governor, and also with Anderson whom he was permitted to visit, that the garrison would soon be withdrawn and that his trip was merely to prepare the way for that event. He left Charleston on the night of the twenty-fifth, arrived in Washington on the twenty-seventh, and reported to Lincoln what he had learned. What had he been sent to Charleston to do? There must have been some purpose and it could hardly have been to prepare the way for Anderson's evacuation. Does it strain the evidence to suggest that it was chiefly to find out at first hand how strong was the Southern feeling about relief for Fort Sumter and that this purpose was camouflaged by the vague intimations of evacuation? But it is quite probable that Lamon himself did not understand the real purpose, for it is altogether unlikely that the cautious Lincoln would have divulged so important a secret to his bibulous and impulsive young friend. But if there was such an ulterior purpose, Lincoln now had the information directly from Charleston that any sort of relief would result in an attack upon the fort.

According to Gideon Welles, whose account of these events was written several years later, Lincoln sometime in the latter half of March had informed the members of his cabinet that he would send relief to Sumter. During a cabinet meeting on March 29 (two days after Lamon's return), when the matter was again discussed, Lincoln, at the suggestion of Attorney General Edward Bates, again requested each member to give his opinion in writing on the question of relieving Sumter. Whether Lincoln's known determination, political pressure, or some other influence had effected it, there was a marked change from the advance given just two weeks earlier. Now only Seward and Caleb Smith were for evacuating Sumter, but they both wished to reinforce Fort Pickens. Bates proposed to strengthen Pickens and Key West and said that the time had come either to evacuate Sumter or relieve it. The rest were unequivocally for a relief expedition. Later that day Lincoln directed the secretaries of War and the Navy to co-operate in preparing an expedition to move by sea as early as April 6. The destination was not indicated in the order, but it was Charleston.

On the same day Seward, intent upon the reinforcement of Fort Pickens, brought Captain M. C. Meigs of the Engineers to Lincoln to discuss an expedition to that place. On March 31 Meigs and Colonel Erasmus D. Keyes, of General Scott's staff, were directed to draw up a plan for the relief of Fort Pickens. They took it to Lincoln who had them take it to Scott to be put into final form and executed. On the next day, April 1, Seward, Meigs, and Lieutenant D. D. Porter of the navy went to the Executive Mansion and after consultation with Lincoln finished the plans for the Pickens expedition. It was to be conducted with such absolute secrecy, lest information leak out to the Confederates, that even the secretaries of War and the Navy were to know

nothing of it. The orders were signed by the President himself. It was only because the same ship, the *Powhatan,* was selected for both expeditions that the Secretary of the Navy learned of the expedition to the Gulf of Mexico. Energetic preparations began in New York and Brooklyn to collect vessels, men, arms, and provisions for the two expeditions.

In the first days of April came the disquieting returns from the elections in Ohio, Connecticut, and Rhode Island. April 4 proved to be an important day. Early that morning Lincoln seems to have had a mysterious conference with a group of Republican governors, said to be seven or nine in number. Among them were Andrew G. Curtin of Pennsylvania, William Dennison of Ohio, Richard Yates of Illinois, Oliver P. Morton of Indiana, Israel Washburn of Maine, and Austin Blair of Michigan. How did all these governors happen to be in Washington at the same time? The newspapers, in so far as they noticed the presence of these gentlemen, assumed that they were looking after patronage; but rumors were soon current that they had gone to demand of the President that he send relief to the garrison at Fort Sumter. This is not improbable since all these men belonged to the aggressive group of Republicans who had been alarmed at the rumors of evacuation and they could hardly have known what Lincoln had already planned. Several questions arise here. If Lincoln was still hesitating, did they bring pressure upon him and force him to a decision? Or did Lincoln allow them to think they were helping him to decide? Or, if the President had not actually summoned them to a conference, did he seize the opportunity to make sure of their powerful support in case the Confederates should show fight? Were mutual pledges of action and support exchanged that morning?

Later that same morning occurred the much-discussed Lincoln-Baldwin interview. On April 2, apparently at the suggestion of Seward, Lincoln had sent Allan B. Magruder, a Virginia Unionist living in Washington, to Richmond to ask G. W. Summers, the leader of the Unionists in the State Convention, to come to see him at once or to send some other representative from that group. Magruder reached Richmond the next day. As Summers could not leave, John B. Baldwin, another leader of the group, was selected; and Baldwin and Magruder were in Washington early on the morning of April 4. They went to Seward who conducted Baldwin to Lincoln at eleven o'clock. Lincoln took Baldwin alone into a bedroom, locked the door and exclaimed "You have come too late!" In the conversation which followed, according to Baldwin's statement, the President asked why the Unionists in the Virginia Convention did not adjourn sine die, as the continuance of the session was a standing menace to him. Baldwin replied that if they should so adjourn without having accomplished anything for the security of the state, another convention would certainly be called and it would be more strongly secessionist. He then urged the President to assure peace to the country and strengthen the border-state Unionists by evacuating both Sumter and Pickens and calling upon the whole people to settle their differences in a national convention. Lincoln replied that his supporters would not permit him to withdraw the garrisons. Baldwin then warned him that if a fight started at Fort Sumter, no matter who started it, war would follow and Virginia would go out of the Union in forty-eight hours. Lincoln became greatly excited and exclaimed, "Why was I not told this a week ago? You have come too late!" This is Baldwin's account, but it is substantiated by several

other Virginia Unionists, at least to the extent that it was what Baldwin told them when he returned to Richmond the next day.

But John Minor Botts, a violent Virginia Unionist who by invitation talked with Lincoln on the night of April 7, insisted that Lincoln then told him that he had offered to Baldwin to withdraw Anderson's force from Sumter if the Virginia Convention would adjourn sine die, that he would gladly swap a fort for a state; but that Baldwin refused the offer. When Botts offered to take the proposition to Richmond at once Lincoln replied, "Oh, it is too late; the fleet has sailed and I have no means of communicating with it."

Baldwin always denied that Lincoln had made any such proposal as Botts reported. Did Baldwin lie? He seems to have had a much better reputation for accuracy than Botts and his account of his journey to Washington is accurate as far as it can be checked, whereas Botts' story is full of minor inaccuracies. Besides, Baldwin was a sincere Unionist and voted against secession to the last. Why should he have refused Lincoln's offer and failed to report it to his fellow Unionists in Richmond? Did Botts lie about what Lincoln told him? His extreme prejudices and frequently unwarranted statements on other matters would easily bring this conclusion into the range of possibility, were it not for the fact that Lincoln seems to have told much the same story to others. If Lincoln did, then the question whether the President offered to evacuate Sumter at this stage of his plan becomes an issue of veracity between Lincoln and Baldwin, which obviously places the Virginian at a great disadvantage. But let us consider other factors in the situation. Lincoln had just been holding conferences with the militant Republican governors and evidently had come to some agreement with them, else why should he greet his visitor with the exclamation, repeated later in the conversation, "You have come too late"? Certainly he could not have referred to the final orders to Fox, for those orders were given later that day. And why did he refuse on the night of April 7, if the Botts story is correct, to permit Botts to take his proposition to Richmond, alleging that the fleet had sailed, when in fact none of the vessels left New York until the next night? Is there not some basis for suspecting that Lincoln had not actually made the offer to Baldwin to evacuate Sumter because he was already bound by some sort of agreement with the Republican governors to send the expedition forward; and that later, desiring above all things to leave the impression that he had done everything in his power to avoid a collision, he dropped hints about an offer which had been flatly refused?

During the afternoon of April 4 Lincoln saw Captain Fox, who was to have charge of the Sumter expedition, and told him of his final determination to send relief to Anderson and that notification of the relief expedition would be sent to the Governor of South Carolina before Fox could possibly arrive off Charleston Harbor. Fox hurried back to New York to push his preparations. At some time that same day Lincoln drafted a letter to Major Anderson, which was copied and signed by the Secretary of War, informing him that relief would be sent him.

On the afternoon of April 6 Secretary Welles received a letter from Captain Henry A. Adams of the navy, stationed off Fort Pickens, explaining that he had not landed the artillery company at the fort in accordance with General Scott's order of March 12 because of controlling orders from the former Secretary of the Navy to respect the truce of February 29, but stating that he was now ready to obey if ordered to land the men. Welles consulted the President and then hurried off Lieutenant John L. Worden with verbal orders to Captain Adams to land the men at once. This incident gave occasion for a strange statement of Lincoln which deserves notice. In his special message to Congress of July 4, he stated that the expedition for the relief of Sumter was first prepared "to be ultimately used or not according to circumstances," and intimated that, if Pickens had been relieved in March, Sumter would have been evacuated, and that it had not been decided to use the expedition until word came that Fort Pickens had not been reinforced in accordance with the order of March 12. The strange thing about this statement is that word was not received from Adams until April 6, while positive orders had been given two days before to Captain Fox to go ahead with his expedition and at the same time Anderson had been notified to expect it. Had Lincoln become confused about the order of these events? It does not seem probable. Or was he, for effect upon public opinion, trying to strengthen the belief that his hand had been forced, that his pacific intentions had been defeated by circumstances?

On April 1 Lincoln had passed the promise through Seward and Justice John A. Campbell to the Confederate Commissioners in Washington that he would notify Governor Pickens if any relief expedition should be sent to Fort Sumter. When they learned of it, several members of his cabinet objected to such notification, but Lincoln insisted; he had his own reasons for so doing. The formal notice which he drafted with his own hand, dated April 6, is interesting not only for its careful phrasing but for the evident importance which he attached to it. It was embodied in a letter of instruction to R. S. Chew, an official of the state department who was to be accompanied by Captain Theodore Talbot, directing him to proceed to Charleston where, if he found that Fort Sumter had not been evacuated or attacked and that the flag was still over it, he was to seek an interview with Governor Pickens, read to him the statement and give him a copy of it. If he found the fort evacuated or attacked he was to seek no interview but was to return forthwith. The message to Governor Pickens was in these words:

I am directed by the President of the United States to notify you to expect an attempt will be made to supply Fort Sumter with provisions only; and that, if such an attempt be not resisted, no effort to throw in men, arms, or ammunition will be made without further notice, or in case of an attack upon the fort.

Was the purpose of this message merely to fulfill a promise? Is there not special significance in the fact that Lincoln entrusted the form of it to no one else, but carefully drafted it himself? It is unnecessary to call attention again to the fact that Lincoln was a rare master of the written word, that he had the skill of an artist in so phrasing a sentence that it conveyed precisely the meaning he wished it to convey. He could do more than that: he could make the same sentence say one thing to one person and something entirely different to another and in each case carry the meaning he intended. It is obvious that the message to be read to Governor Pickens was intended less for that official than for General Beauregard and the Confederate government at Montgomery. But it was intended also for the people of the North and of the border states. To the suspicious and apprehensive Confederates it did not merely give information

that provisions would be sent to Anderson's garrison—which should be enough to bring about an attempt to take the fort—but it carried a threat that force would be used if the provisions were not allowed to be brought in. It was a direct challenge! How were the Southerners expected to react to this challenge? To Northern readers the same words meant only that the government was taking food to hungry men to whom it was under special obligation. Northern men would see no threat; they would understand only that their government did not propose to use force if it could be avoided. Is it possible that a man of Lincoln's known perspicacity could be blind to the different interpretations which would be placed upon his subtle words in the North and in the South?

The message was not only skillfully phrased, it was most carefully timed. It was read to Governor Pickens in the presence of General Beauregard on the evening of April 8. News of the preparation of some large expedition had been in the newspapers for a week; but as the destination had not been officially divulged, newspaper reporters and correspondents had guessed at many places, chiefly the coast of Texas and revolutionary Santo Domingo. It was not until April 8 that the guessing veered toward Charleston, and not until the next day was any positive information given in the press of the notice to Governor Pickens. The Confederate officials had regarded these preparations at New York with suspicion while conflicting reports came to them from Washington concerning Lincoln's designs about Sumter. The first of Captain Fox's vessels were leaving New York Harbor at the very hour that Chew read the notification to Governor Pickens. The Confederates were given ample time, therefore, to act before the fleet could arrive off Charleston. They did not know that a portion of the vessels which had left New York were really destined not for Charleston but for Fort Pickens at Pensacola. The utmost secrecy was maintained about the Pensacola expedition, thus permitting the Confederates to believe that the whole force was to be concentrated at Charleston.

The tables were now completely turned on the Southerners. Lincoln was well out of his dilemma while they, who had heretofore had the tactical advantage of being able to wait until Anderson must evacuate, were suddenly faced with a choice of two evils. They must either take the fort before relief could arrive, thus taking the apparent offensive which they had hoped to avoid, or they must stand by quietly and see the fort provisioned. But to allow the provisioning meant not only an indefinite postponement to their possession of the fort which had become as much a symbol to them as it was to Lincoln; to permit it in the face of the threat of force, after all their preparations, would be to make a ridiculous and disgraceful retreat. Nor could they be sure that, if they yielded now in the matter of "provisions only," they would not soon be served with the "further notice" as a prelude to throwing in "men, arms, and ammunition." This, then, was the dilemma which they faced as the result of Lincoln's astute strategy.

Events now hurried to the inevitable climax. As soon as President Lincoln's communication was received General Beauregard telegraphed the news to the Confederate secretary of war, L. P. Walker. Walker at once ordered that the Sumter garrison be isolated by stopping its mails and the purchase of provisions in Charleston. On this same day the Confederate commissioners at Washington had received a copy of a memorandum filed in the state department by Seward, dated March 15, in which the Secretary declined to hold any official intercourse with them. They telegraphed the news to their government and at once, feeling that they had been deceived and knowing that their mission had failed, prepared to leave Washington. Jefferson Davis was thus, on April 8, apprised of two movements by the Federal government which, taken together or singly, looked ominous. On the following day Beauregard seized the mails as they came from Fort Sumter and discovered a letter from Anderson to the war department which disclosed that he had been informed of the coming of Fox's expedition and indicated that the fleet would attempt to force its way into the harbor. This information also was at once communicated to the Montogomery government. On the tenth came the news that the fleet had sailed from New York. Walker then directed Beauregard, if he thought there was no doubt of the authorized character of the notification from Washington (meaning Lincoln's), to demand the evacuation of Fort Sumter and, if it should be refused, "to reduce" the fort. The Davis administration had waited two full days after receiving word of Lincoln's notification before deciding what to do. It is said that Robert Toombs, secretary of state, objected vigorously to attacking the fort. "It is unnecessary; it puts us in the wrong; it is fatal!" If Toombs protested, he was overruled because Davis and the rest believed that Lincoln had already taken the aggressive and they regarded their problem now as a military one. To them it was the simple question whether they should permit the hostile fleet to arrive before they attacked the fort or whether they should take Sumter before they had to fight both fort and fleet.

At two o'clock on the eleventh Beauregard made the demand upon Anderson, who rejected it but added verbally to the officer sent to him that if not battered to pieces, he would be starved out in a few days. When Beauregard reported this remark to Walker, that official informed him that the government did "not desire needlessly to bombard Fort Sumter" and that if Major Anderson would state when he would evacuate, Beauregard should "avoid the effusion of blood." Evidently the Montgomery officials thought there was still a chance to get the fort peaceably before the fleet could arrive. Had not Lincoln so carefully timed his message with the movement of Fox there might have been no attack. But late in the afternoon of the same day Beauregard received information from a scout boat that the *Harriet Lane,* one of Fox's ships, had been sighted a few miles out of the harbor. It was expected that all the fleet would be at hand by next day. Nevertheless, Beauregard about midnight sent a second message to Anderson, in accordance with Walker's instructions, saying that if he would state the time at which he would evacuate and would agree not to use "your guns against us unless ours should be employed against Fort Sumter, we will abstain from opening fire upon you." To this Anderson replied that he would evacuate by noon on the fifteenth and would in the meantime not open fire upon Beauregard's forces unless compelled to do so by some hostile act "against this fort or the flag it bears, should I not receive prior to that time controlling instructions from my government or additional supplies." This answer was conditional and unsatisfactory for it was clear that, with Fox's fleet arriving, Anderson would not evacuate. Thereupon the two aides who had carried Beauregard's message, in accordance with their instructions from that

officer, formally notified Anderson—it was now 3:20 in the morning of the twelfth—that fire would be opened upon him in one hour's time.

What followed we all know. The bombardment which began at 4:30 on the morning of April 12 ended in the surrender of Anderson and his garrison during the afternoon of the following day. The three vessels of the fleet which lay outside were unable to get into the harbor because of the high seas and the failure of the rest of the fleet—the tugboats and the *Powhatan*—to arrive. Although there were no casualties during the bombardment, the mere news that the attack on the fort had begun swept the entire North into a roaring flame of anger. The "rebels" had fired the first shot; they had chosen to begin war. If there had been any doubt earlier whether the mass of the Northern people would support the administration in suppressing the secessionists, there was none now. Lincoln's strategy had been completely successful. He seized at once the psychological moment for calling out the militia and committing the North to support of the war. This action cost him four of the border slave states, but he had probably already discounted that loss.

Perhaps the facts thus far enumerated, standing alone, could hardly be conclusive evidence that Lincoln, having decided that there was not other way than war for the salvation of his administration, his party, and the Union, maneuvered the Confederates into firing the first shot in order that they, rather than he, should take the blame of beginning bloodshed. Though subject to that interpretation, they are also subject to the one which he built up so carefully. Is there other evidence? No one, surely, would expect to find in any written word of his a confession of the strategem; for to acknowledge it openly would have been to destroy the very effect he had been at so much pains to produce. There are, it is true, two statements by him to Captain Fox which are at least suggestive. Fox relates that in their conference of April 4 the President told him that he had decided to let the expedition go and that a messenger would be sent to the authorities at Charleston before Fox could possibly get there; and when the Captain reminded the President of the short time in which he must organize the expedition and reach the destined point, Lincoln replied, "You will best fulfill your duty to your country by making the attempt." Then, again, in the letter which Lincoln wrote the chagrined Captain on May 1 to console him for the failure of the fleet to enter Charleston Harbor, he said: "You and I both anticipated that the cause of the country would be advanced by making the attempt to provision Fort Sumter, even if it should fail; and it is no small consolation now to feel that our anticipation is justified by the result." Was this statement merely intended to soothe a disappointed commander, or did it contain a hint that the real objective of the expedition was not at all the relief of Sumter?

Lincoln's two secretaries, John G. Nicolay and John Hay, in their long but not impartial account of the Sumter affair come so close to divulging the essence of the stratagem that one cannot but suspect that they knew of it. In one place they say, with reference to Lincoln's solution of this problem of Sumter, "Abstractly it was enough that the Government was in the right. But to make the issue sure, he determined that in addition the rebellion should be put in the wrong." And again, "President Lincoln in deciding the Sumter question had adopted a simple but effective policy. To use his own words, he

determined to 'send bread to Anderson'; if the rebels fired on that, they would not be able to convince the world that he had begun the civil war." And still later, "When he finally gave the order that the fleet should sail he was master of the situation . . . master if the rebels hesitated or repented, because they would thereby forfeit their prestige with the South; master if they persisted, for he would then command a united North."

Perhaps not much weight should be given to the fact that before the expedition reached Charleston his political opponents in the North expressed suspicion of a design to force civil war upon the country in order to save the Republican party from the disasters threatened in the recent elections and that after the fighting began they roundly accused him of having deliberately provoked it by his demonstration against Charleston. And perhaps there is no significance in the further fact that the more aggressive members of his own party had demanded action to save the party and that the administration newspapers began to assert as soon as the fleet sailed that, if war came, the rebels would be the aggressors.

There is evidence much more to the point than any of these things. Stephen A. Douglas, senator from Illinois, died on June 3, 1861. On June 12 the Republican governor of that state, Richard Yates, appointed to the vacancy Orville H. Browning, a prominent lawyer, a former Whig, then an ardent Republican, and for more than twenty years a personal friend of Abraham Lincoln. Browning was one of the group who from the first had favored vigorous measures and had opposed compromise. He was to become the spokesman of the administration in the Senate. On July 2, 1861, Browning arrived in Washington to take his seat in the Senate for the special session which had been called to meet on July 4. On the evening of the third he called at the White House to see his old acquaintance. Now Browning for many years had kept a diary, a fact that very probably was unknown to Lincoln since diarists usually conceal this pleasant and useful vice. In the entry for July 3 Browning relates the conversation he had with the President that evening, for after reading the new Senator his special message to Congress, Lincoln laid aside the document and talked. The rest of the entry had best be given in Browning's own words:

He told me that the very first thing placed in his hands after his inauguration was a letter from Majr Anderson announcing the impossibility of defending or relieving Sumter. That he called the cabinet together and consulted Genl Scott—that Scott concurred with Anderson, and the cabinet, with the exception of P M Genl Blair were for evacuating the Fort, and all the troubles and anxieties of his life had not equalled those which intervened between this time and the fall of Sumter. He himself conceived the idea, and proposed sending supplies, without an attempt to reinforce giving notice of the fact to Gov Pickens of S.C. The plan succeeded. They attacked Sumter—it fell, and thus, did more service than it otherwise could.

This statement, condensed from the words of Lincoln himself by a close friend who wrote them down when he returned that night to his room at "Mrs. Carter's on Capitol Hill," needs no elaboration. It completes the evidence.

It is not difficult to understand how the usually secretive Lincoln, so long surrounded by strangers and criticized by many whom he had expected to be helpful, talking that night for the first time in many months to an old, loyal, and discreet friend, though a friend who had often been somewhat patronizing, for once forgot to be reticent. It must have been an emotional relief to him, with his pride over his consummate strategy bottled up within him for so long, to be able to impress his friends Browning with his success in meeting a perplexing and dangerous situation. He did not suspect that Browning would set it down in a diary.

There is little more to be said. Some of us will be content to find new reason for admiration of Abraham Lincoln in reflecting on this bit of masterful strategy at the very beginning of his long struggle for the preservation of the Union. Some, perhaps, will be reminded of the famous incident of the Ems telegram of which the cynical Bismarck boasted in his memoirs. And some will wonder whether the sense of responsibility for the actual beginning of a frightful war, far more terrible than he could possibly have foreseen in that early April of 1861, may have deepened the melancholy and the charity toward his Southern foemen which that strange man in the White House was to reveal so often before that final tragic April of 1865.

Unlike Ramsdell, the distinguished Lincoln scholar DAVID M. POTTER (1910–   ), who was born in Georgia and has taught in the South, at Yale, and at Stanford University, absolves the President from the charge of having provoked the Confederacy. In the following excerpts from the preface to the 1962 edition of his book, originally published in 1942, he reaffirms his conviction that Lincoln sought to preserve peace rather than to provoke war when he ordered the expedition for the relief of the beleaguered fort. How does Potter refute Ramsdell? Does his argument exculpate the President?*

David M. Potter

Lincoln's Peaceful Intentions

Along with the debate as to what policy ought to have been adopted in 1861, there is also a disagreement as to what policy actually was adopted, for there has been a spirited dispute concerning the real intent of the Lincoln administration. This brings me to the second controversial aspect of my study. My narrative emphasized the idea that Lincoln wanted peace and believed until the last moment that he might be able to preserve it. Many very able historians, like Bruce Catton, David Donald, and Allan Nevins, hold a similar view, but there are other scholars whose work must be taken very seriously who deny that Lincoln wanted peace or, if not that he wanted it, that he either expected it or thought it practicable to seek.

When I wrote in 1942, the chief exponent of this view was the late Professor Charles W. Ramsdell. Ramsdell, a Texan and a man of Southern sympathies, took a fairly clear-cut position. Lincoln, he said, was in a dilemma from which he perceived that he could escape if the Southerners "could . . . be *induced* [his italics] to attack Sumter." Therefore Lincoln deliberately "maneuvered the Confederates into firing the first shot." He adopted a "stratagem," and when Sumter was fired upon he knew that his "strategy had been completely successful." Ramsdell compared Lincoln's handling of the Sumter situation to Bismarck's handling of the Ems telegram. . . .

A few years after Ramsdell's paper,

*David M. Potter, *Lincoln and His Party in the Secession Crisis* 2d ed., (New Haven: Yale University Press, 1962), pp. xxiii–xxxii. (Footnotes omitted). Reprinted by permission of Yale University Press.

Kenneth M. Stampp published another interpretation of Lincoln's policy, which was formulated in his paper entitled "Lincoln and the Strategy of Defense in 1861" and in his book *And the War Came. . . .* Stampp's argument was a subtle and balanced one, less easy to summarize than Ramsdell's, but he seemed to say first that, without really wanting war, Lincoln *expected war* — he saw it was on the way, and he prepared not to be caught at a disadvantage by its coming; and second, that without actually *inducing* (Ramsdell's word) the Confederates to start a war, Lincoln took a position to which he foresaw the Confederates would react by starting a war. In Stampp's opinion, Lincoln was quite satisfied with the outcome. Both writers spoke of Lincoln's action as a "maneuver," and Stampp spoke distinctly of Lincoln's "coercionist views," and of his policy as one of "casting coercion in the mold of defense." According to Stampp, Lincoln saw the possibilities in the situation where "the Union government could easily pretend to forego aggressive action and simulate a defensive pose."

It would be a neat question to determine wherein Ramsdell and Stampp agreed, and wherein they disagreed. Certainly Ramsdell laid emphasis upon the thought that Lincoln actually desired war, while Stampp stressed the thought that he accepted it as something that could not be averted and must be handled in an advantageous way. Also, Ramsdell pictured him as scheming to provoke the Confederates to attack, while Stampp portrays him rather as taking a position which he shrewdly foresaw that they would attack. But these differences sometimes blur at the edges, and to some extent both writers are saying the same things: Lincoln concluded that he could only save the Union by means of war; he perceived that it would be greatly to his advantage if the adversary did the first shooting; he therefore worked out a policy at Fort Sumter which he clearly foresaw would result in an initiation of hostilities by the Confederates; his claims of a peaceful intent merely to provision the fort were disingenuous; and when war came, he was well satisfied with the result.

The most substantial difference between Ramsdell and Stampp clearly turns not upon what they think Lincoln was doing but upon how they feel about what they think he was doing. Ramsdell, with his Southern sympathies, was shocked and disapproving. Stampp, on the contrary, with solidly Northern sympathies, says in effect that the War was worth what it cost, that it had to be, and that Lincoln is to be admired for putting his adversaries in the wrong and for facing up to the situation without shirking it.

Professor Stampp is a most resourceful scholar, and so is Richard N. Current, who has to some extent associated himself with Stampp's position. They make an impressive presentation. For instance, Stampp adduces a very strong argument that Lincoln must have known that war was likely to result from sending provisions to Sumter. He knew that the Confederates had fired on the *Star of the West* when it brought provisions; members of the cabinet told him plainly that the sending of provisions would result in war; and, as Current emphasizes, his special emissary to Charleston, Stephen A. Hurlbut, reported to him on March 17 that any attempt to send provisions would result in war.

It is certainly true, as Stampp and Current contend, that Lincoln must have seen the likelihood of war, and that his thought must have reckoned with that contingency. I now believe that I should have recognized this fact more clearly and explicitly than I did, and if I were rewriting my account now, I would do so. But for reasons which I will indicate further on, it seems to me that, whatever other effects his recognition of the increasing likelihood of war may have had upon Lincoln, it did not cause him to deviate a single step from a course of action which can be precisely defined. This course was to avoid any menacing action or any action which might precipitate a clash, just as far as was possible consistently with maintaining the principle of Union. As I have argued at some length, ... Lincoln pointedly refrained from the exercise of all the customary forms of federal authority in the seceded states, any of which he would have been perfectly justified in asserting.

Not all of Stampp's and Current's arguments seem to me as convincing as their demonstration that Lincoln must have realized the increasing likelihood of war. For instance, they have made very detailed computations to discredit Lincoln's statement in his message to Congress in July 1861 that he had decided upon sending the final expedition to Fort Sumter only after his attempt to reinforce Fort Pickens had failed. He stated that he had wanted to demonstrate, by the reinforcement of Pickens, "a clear indication of policy," and that if he had been able to do this it would have "better enable[d] the country to accept the evacuation of Fort Sumter as a military necessity." Stampp's analysis emphasizes, quite correctly, that Lincoln had certainly ordered the Sumter expedition prepared before he learned that the reinforcement of Pickens had miscarried. It also emphasizes the even more important points that Lincoln had actually gone to the length of ordering the expedition to move, and of sending word to Major Anderson that it would move. But it is crucial that the evidence still indicates that Lincoln did not inform the

Governor of South Carolina that the Sumter expedition would be sent until exactly the time when news reached Washington that the orders of March 11 for the reinforcing of Pickens had not been carried out. This news left Pensacola on April 1 and arrived at Washington on April 6, the same day on which Lincoln's message to the Governor of South Carolina was sent. The labored nature of Stampp's and Current's arguments on this point makes it all the more striking that they have found the essential point unassailable: the one irrevocable step, the message to the Governor, was taken on the very day when news arrived of the failure to reinforce Pickens. The first ships of the Sumter expedition did not leave port until two days later.

The assertions, therefore, that Lincoln's later statement about this matter is "scarcely consistent with the known facts" and that "the President had dealt with Sumter and Pickens as separate problems" seem to me arbitrary and insufficiently proved. Also it seems unsatisfactory to say that Lincoln did not need to wait for news of the reinforcement of Pickens, since he "had no reason to doubt that his order would be executed." In fact, his order instructed Union troops to occupy a position which he knew that Confederate forces might try to prevent them from occupying, and he had very real reason to await the result with anxiety. And, of course, his order was not executed, though the Fort was later reinforced.

Another case in point is the question of Lincoln's offer to the Virginians to evacuate Fort Sumter if they would adjourn the Virginia Convention. Historians have fallen into an endless dispute over the insoluble question whether Lincoln made such an offer to John B. Baldwin. But this focus upon Baldwin is unfortunate, for the testimony of Governor Morehead of Kentucky and of John Hay, reporting the statement of Lincoln himself, has long given evidence that Lincoln did propose to the Border State men terms on which he would abandon the Fort. . . . Since the opening of the Lincoln Papers, new evidence in the form of a letter from George Plumer Smith to John Hay on January 9, 1863, asking Hay to secure Lincoln's confirmation of the fact that Lincoln had told him (Smith) of the offer to Baldwin, and a reply from Hay to Smith on January 10 giving this confirmation, tend to corroborate this further. Professor Stampp deals with this evidence by doubting that Lincoln "seriously expected the Virginians to accept the offer," and Professor Current by saying that "these letters, it seems to me, by no means settle the controversy as to whether Lincoln actually made an offer to give up the fort."

There is certainly a substantial amount of evidence, whether it is conclusive or not, both in general terms and in specific terms, that Lincoln thought, until very late in the crisis, if not until the end, that he could achieve both peace and Union and would not have to choose between them. In this connection it is important to remember how consistently the Republicans had ridiculed all threats of secession, and how much they were the captives of their own mental set when secession came. In the light of this mental set, it is not really necessary to attribute such adroit hidden purposes as Stampp attributes to Lincoln in explaining his statement that "there is no crisis but an artificial one."

It is also important to remember that in some respects the secession movement, as of March 1861, had failed and that Seward, at least, regarded it as a failure. Eight slave states were still in the Union; only seven had seceded. The secessionists had been beaten in Virginia, North Caro-

lina, Tennessee, Arkansas, and Missouri, and the efforts to create a united South had divided the South as never before.

Another point which it is essential to keep in view if Lincoln's thinking is to be understood is that the President-elect made all his calculations, until March 5, on the assumption that Major Anderson's position at Fort Sumter was secure and that the existing status could continue for some time without any positive action on the part of the new administration. Not until March 5 did Secretary Holt and General Scott confront him with the news that a decision would have to be made at once either to abandon Fort Sumter or to take positive action for the support of the Fort.

Without being repetitious about evidence which is discussed more fully in the main body of this work, I would argue also that there are several items of evidence which indicate that Lincoln did quite seriously consider the evacuation of Fort Sumter. For instance: the fact that he made overtures to the Virginians about this possibility; the fact that Seward expected evacuation with enough confidence to make promises to the Confederates, based upon the expectation; the fact that Trumbull feared evacuation enough to introduce monitory resolutions in the Senate reminding the new head of the Republican party of his duty "to hold and protect the public property." Could these things have happened if the idea of evacuation had not seemed very much a reality?

The dispute concerning evidence, however, could go on endlessly for two reasons. First, because there were large factors working toward war and large factors working for peace, and both left a substantial residue of evidence. Thus one can marshal extensive material to show the magnitude of the demands upon Lincoln to hold Sumter or the extent of the pressure upon him to evacuate the Fort. Applying this ambivalence to Lincoln's own situation, one can legitimately stress his seeming expectation in March that he would abandon Sumter, or one can with equal validity emphasize the deep reluctance with which he arrived at this expectation. The historian can show that many of Lincoln's contemporaries regarded the first inaugural address as a threat of coercion, or he can show that many others thought it was too mild and was a promise of peace. That this disagreement continues is evident from the fact that, in our own time, Stampp sees it primarily as a statement "in which he [Lincoln] took such enormous pains to absolve himself from the charge of aggression," while Allan Nevins sees it as "one long plea for patience, forebearance, and the avoidance of rash action," and Roy F. Nichols calls it "a stirring plea to avoid hostilities."

A second reason that the review of evidence can never be conclusive is that the dispute turns not only upon what Lincoln did but upon what he thought. In other words, it is a question of motive as well as of action. Motive lies to a considerable extent beyond historical proof, partly because historical judgments must depend upon acts, and the same act may be performed with diverse motives by different persons. Thus a man may perform an act which is honest in its effect because he is an honest man on principle, or because he wants whatever policy will prove most advantageous to him and he believes that honesty is the best policy. This example is not far from the point at issue here, for essentially I am arguing that Lincoln followed a peaceable-seeming course because he was a peaceable man who wanted peace and thought he could attain it. Stampp and Current are essentially arguing that he wanted an effective policy, knew that a peaceable-seeming policy

would be most effective, and therefore took care to make his policy appear peaceable, though there was a covert element of coercion and of aggressiveness in it. They contend that he did not really mind fighting a war to protect the national interest.

If motive cannot be accurately determined, there will always be room both for the beliefs that Lincoln's purposes were peaceable or, alternatively, that the peaceable appearance of his position cloaked a purpose far from pacific. But if the question of motive must, by its very nature, be forever open to doubt, it becomes doubly important to turn back to the question of actions. At this level, the historian faces a different problem: given Lincoln's determination to save the Union, and given his belief that the loss of Fort Sumter, without being sure of Fort Pickens, would make it impossible to save the Union, could he have followed any more peaceable course than he did? Was there any possible means of holding Sumter that would have been less provocative than informing the Confederates that "an attempt will be made to supply Fort Sumter with provisions only and that if such attempt be not resisted, no effort to throw in men, arms, or ammunition will be made, without further notice or [except] in case of an attack upon the Fort." The existence of such an alternative and the demonstration that Lincoln rejected it is essential to any argument that Lincoln was not following the most peaceable course available to him.

Unless the historians who charge Lincoln with coercive or covertly aggressive policies can name a less provocative course that he might have followed, they are in the curious position of arguing that a man may pursue a course which offers the maximum possibility of peace and may at the same time be open to the accusation of scheming to bring about war.

If the very nature of human motivation

is such that no one can ever say categorically whether Lincoln's purposes were peaceable, perhaps it is more nearly possible to say categorically whether his course of action was peaceable. Here the crucial fact is that no one who attributes to him a purpose to see that the war got started in a way that would be advantageous to him has yet said what else he could have done that would have been more peaceable than what he did, given his purpose not to abandon the principle of Union.

No doubt he must have recognized that war might ensue; no doubt he must have seen that if it did ensue, it would come in a way disadvantageous to the Confederacy; no doubt he was glad this was true. But when we say this, we are back in the realm of motive again. If we confine ourselves to scrutinizing his overt course, the question persists: what could he have done that would have been more peaceable? Two outstanding scholars have defined this point well. J. G. Randall stated it with superb precision when he wrote: "To say that Lincoln meant that the first shot would be fired by the other side, *if a first shot was fired* [Randall's italics], is by no means the equivalent of saying that he deliberately maneuvered to have the shot fired. This distinction is fundamental." Allan Nevins stated it with wonderful force when he said: "'In your hands, not mine,' he [Lincoln] had told Southerners, 'lies the issue of peace or war.' The shells that burst over a Federal fort awaiting a victualizing expedition which had orders not to fire unless it was fired upon, gave the answer to that statement."

RICHARD N. CURRENT (1912–   ), Distinguished
Professor at the University of North Carolina at
Greensboro, offers still another interpretation of
Lincoln's motives. Faced with the dilemma of the
rapidly worsening situation at Fort Sumter, the
President, deciding to send only supplies to Major
Anderson and to warn the South Carolina authorities
of his intentions, according to Current's account, took
a deliberate risk. How does the following selection from
his book, *Lincoln and the First Shot,* refute Potter's
thesis?*

Richard N. Current

Lincoln's Risky Gamble

To most Northerners of the Civil War
generation, it seemed obvious that the
Southerners had started the war. The
Southerners had fired the first shot and,
what was worse, had done so without real
provocation. They had begun the bloodshed on being informed that the Federal
government would attempt to carry food
to a few dozen hungry and beleaguered
men.

To certain Northerners, however, and
to practically all Southerners, it seemed
just as obvious that Lincoln was to blame.
While the war was still going on, one
New York Democrat confided to another
his suspicion that Lincoln had brought
off an "adroit manoeuver" to "precipitate
the attack" for its "expected effect upon

the public feeling of the North." A one-
time Kentucky governor, speaking in
Liverpool, England, stated that the Republicans had schemed to "provoke a collision in order that they might say that the
Confederates had made the first attack."
The Richmond journalist E. A. Pollard
wrote in his wartime history of the war
that Lincoln had "procured" the assault
and thus, by an "ingenious artifice," had
himself commenced the fighting. "He
chose to draw the sword," the *Petersburg
Express* asserted, "but by a dirty trick succeeded in throwing upon the South the
seeming blame of firing the first gun."

When, soon after the war's end, Alexander H. Stephens wrote his memoirs,
he had no doubt as to who the real aggres-

*From the book *Lincoln and the First Shot* by Richard N. Current, pp. 182–208. Copyright, ©, 1963 by
Richard N. Current. Reprinted by permission of J. B. Lippincott Company. (Footnotes omitted).

sor had been in 1861. In the book he conducted an imaginary colloquium. "Do you mean to say, Mr. Stephens, that the war was inaugurated by Mr. Lincoln?" he had one of his listeners ask. "Most assuredly I do," Stephens replied. "Why, how in the world . . . ?" the incredulous one persisted. "It is a fact that the *first gun* was fired by the Confederates," Stephens conceded. Then he patiently explained that the aggressor in a war is not the first to use force but the first to make force necessary.

Jefferson Davis, in his account of *The Rise and Fall of the Confederate Government* (1881), agreed with Stephens on this point, though he had agreed with him on little else while the two were president and vice president of the Confederacy. "He who makes the assault is not necessarily he who strikes the first blow or fires the first gun," Davis wrote. Referring to the Republicans and the Sumter expedition, he elaborated: "To have awaited further strengthening of their position by land and naval forces, with hostile purpose now declared, would have been as unwise as it would be to hesitate to strike down the arm of the assailant, who levels a deadly weapon at one's breast, until he has actually fired."

Some Northerners, defenders of Lincoln, took a view rather similar to that of his Southern critics but presented it in a very different light. They praised Lincoln for essentially the same reasons that Davis, Stephens, and others blamed him.

In a book (1882) purporting to give the "true stories" of Sumter and Pickens, and dedicated to the "old friends" of Robert Anderson, a lieutenant colonel of the United States Army maintained that the advice of Scott and Seward to withdraw from Sumter was quite sound from a merely military standpoint. "But Mr. Lincoln and Mr. Blair judged more

wisely that it would be better to sacrifice the garrison of Sumter for political effect." They sent the expedition "with the knowledge that it would compel the rebels to strike the first blow. If the last man in the garrison of Sumter had perished, it would have been a cheap price to pay for the magnificent outburst of patriotism that followed."

In their ten-volume history (1890) Lincoln's former private secretaries, John G. Nicolay and John Hay, wrote that Lincoln cared little whether the Sumter expedition would succeed in its provisioning attempt. "He was not playing a game of military strategy with Beauregard." He was playing a game for much higher stakes than Sumter itself. "When he finally gave the order that the fleet should sail he was master of the situation . . . master if the rebels hesitated or repented, because they would thereby forfeit their prestige with the South; master if they persisted, for he would then command a united North." He was "looking through and beyond the Sumter expedition to the now inevitable rebel attack and the response of an awakened and united North." The government, of course, was in the right. "But to make the issue sure, he determined in addition that the rebellion should be put in the wrong." His success entitled him to the high honors of "universal statesmanship."

In later generations a number of writers repeated the view that Lincoln himself had compelled the Confederates to fire first. Most of these writers inclined to the opinion that, in doing so, he exhibited less of universal statesmanship than of low cunning. Not till 1935, however, did a professional historian present a forthright statement of the thesis with all the accouterments of scholarship. In that year Professor Charles W. Ramsdell, of the University of Texas, reading a paper at the annual meeting of the American Historical Association, thus summed up the case:

"Lincoln, having decided that there was no other way than war for the salvation of his administration, his party, and the Union, maneuvered the Confederates into firing the first shot in order that they, rather than he, should take the blame of beginning bloodshed."

According to the Ramsdell argument, Davis and the rest of the Confederate leaders desired peace. They were eager to negotiate a settlement and avoid a resort to arms. But Lincoln, not so peaceably inclined, refused to deal with them.

During the weeks that followed his inauguration he was beset on two sides. Coercionists demanded that he take forceful action to rescue Fort Sumter. Moderate men advised him to yield the fort. If he should use force, he might impel the states of the Upper South to secede, and perhaps the border states as well. If he should abandon the fort, the majority of his party would probably abandon him. While he hesitated, his fellow Republicans bickered among themselves, his administration declined in prestige, and the country drifted toward ruin. He had to make up his mind soon, before the Sumter garrison was starved out.

At last he hit upon a way out of his dilemma. The thought occurred to him— *must have* occurred to him—that he could induce the Confederates to attack the fort. Then, the flag having been fired upon, he would gain all the benefits of an aroused patriotism. Republicans and Democrats would forget their quarrels of party and faction, the border states would respond with an upsurge of loyalty, and wavering millions throughout the North would rally to the Union cause. The party, the administration, and the Union would be saved.

The stratagem was a shrewd one, worthy of the shrewd man that Lincoln was. He decided to send the expedition and—most cleverly—to give advance notice. A genius with words, he could make them mean different things to different people. This is what he did with the words he addressed to the governor of South Carolina. To Northerners these words would seem quite innocent. The government was taking groceries to starving men and would not use force unless it had to. That was all. To Southerners the same words carried a threat, indeed a double threat. First, Sumter was going to be provisioned so that it could hold out. Second, if resistance should be offered, arms and men as well as food were going to be run in!

The notice was timed as carefully as it was phrased. It was delivered while the ships of the expedition were departing from New York. These could not reach their destination for three days at least, and so the Confederates would have plenty of time to take counteraction before the ships arrived. Already the Confederates had news that a sizable expedition was being prepared, and they were left to suppose that the entire force (including the part of it actually being dispatched to Pensacola) was heading for Charleston. With such a large force presumed to be on the way, they had all the more reason to move quickly.

The ruse worked perfectly. True, the expedition neither provisioned nor reinforced Sumter; it gave the garrison no help at all. But that was not the object. The object was to provoke a shot that would rouse the Northern people to fight.

This Ramsdell thesis was elaborated, with variations, in a book written by a Southern lawyer, John S. Tilley, and published during that fateful year 1941 (when another President was to be accused of a first-shot "maneuver"). Writing in a spirit more appropriate to a criminal court than a scholarly forum, Tilley contended that, at the time of Lincoln's inauguration, there existed no real need for provisioning Sumter. Indeed, Tilley left the impression that Lincoln had invented the story of short supplies at the fort so as to have an excuse for forcing the issue with the Confederacy. One of Tilley's chapter titles announced: "Lincoln Got What He Wanted." The implication was that Lincoln wanted war and went out of his way to get it.

While the Ramsdell thesis has attracted other and more responsible adherents, it has also been challenged by formidable critics. Professor James G. Randall, of the University of Illinois, maintained in the *Abraham Lincoln Quarterly* (1940) and in two books on Lincoln (1945, 1947) that Lincoln intended and expected a peaceful provisioning of the fort. After an independent study of *Lincoln and His Party in the Secession Crisis* (1942), Professor David M. Potter, then of Yale University (now of Stanford University), presented essentially similar conclusions. Lincoln counted upon a resurgence of Unionism in the South to overcome secession eventually, without war. To facilitate reunion, he planned to refrain from forcible assertion of Federal authority so long as he could do so without an obvious and outright surrender of it. He would have evacuated Fort Sumter if he had been able promptly enough to reinforce and secure Fort Pickens, so that it could serve as a substitute symbol of Federal authority. Events, however, compelled him to act. Finally he accepted the necessity of the Sumter expedition, but he took care to make it as unprovocative as possible. By means of it he hoped merely to preserve the existing status in Charleston Harbor. His policy was a failure, since it culmi-

nated in war. Such is the contention of Professors Randall and Potter.

In between the Randall-Potter thesis of the peace policy and the Ramsdell-Tilley thesis of the war maneuver, there is yet a third interpretation which sees Lincoln's policy as aiming at neither war nor peace, as such, but as risking the chance of war. Professor Kenneth M. Stampp, of the University of California, stated this thesis of the calculated risk in the *Journal of Southern History* (1945) and restated it in his book *And the War Came* (1950). According to Stampp, Lincoln's primary purpose was to preserve the Union and to do so by a "strategy of defense" which would avoid even the appearance of initiating hostilities.

One version of the Sumter story—Tilley's insinuation that Lincoln faked the hunger crisis at the fort—may be immediately ruled out. This insinuation was based mainly upon the absence of evidence. Tilley could not find the letter, or even a copy of the letter, that Lincoln was supposed to have seen on the day after his inauguration, the letter in which Major Anderson revealed shortages of certain essential supplies and the necessity of either replenishing these or abandoning the fort. Now, it may be good legal practice to argue from the absence of evidence. It is not sound historical scholarship. Even at the time Tilley wrote, there were documents available referring to the Anderson letter and indicating clearly enough that it actually had been written and sent. Later, after the opening of the Robert Todd Lincoln Collection of Lincoln papers in the Library of Congress, in 1947, lo! there was the missing letter which Tilley had been at such pains to prove nonexistent.

The Ramsdell thesis itself does not necessarily fall with the collapse of Tilley's case, though much of Ramsdell's evidence is either inconclusive or irrelevant. He devoted a considerable part of his essay merely to showing that various pressures or supposed pressures had induced Lincoln to decide in favor of sending the Sumter expedition, but this line of argument has little bearing upon the main issue to which Ramsdell had addressed himself. As his critic Randall aptly commented: "The inducing-to-attack argument does not proceed very far before it involves a subtle change of approach, so that the very decision to send the expedition is treated as the aggressive or provocative thing, whereas the point at issue . . . is whether the sending of supplies to feed the garrison was not in Lincoln's mind compatible with continued peace efforts."

This is indeed a crucial question. It may be restated thus: Did Lincoln think, or did he have good reason to think, that he could send his expedition to Sumter and his advance notice to the South Carolina governor without encountering resistance on the part of the Confederate forces at Charleston? Unfortunately, there is no direct, contemporary evidence to show what Lincoln *actually thought* about the probable Confederate reaction. There is, however, plenty of evidence to indicate what he *had good reason to think.*

Lincoln was familiar with the news of recent events at Charleston—events illustrating the readiness of the Confederate batteries to open up. He knew that in January his predecessor, President Buchanan, had sent an unescorted and unarmed merchant steamer with provisions and (below deck) troops for Sumter, and that the Charleston batteries had fired upon this vessel and compelled her to turn back. Now, Lincoln was sending not one ship but several, including warships. He had reason to expect that his expedi-

tion would meet with at least the same degree of hostility as Buchanan's had met with, if not more. Before Lincoln's expedition had actually sailed, he received confirmation of this probability in the report that, on April 3, the Confederate batteries fired upon the Boston schooner *R. H. Shannon,* which innocently had put in at Charleston Harbor to get out of the ocean fog.

When Lincoln called upon his cabinet for written advice, on March 15 and again on March 29, he got little assurance the first time and still less the second time that a peaceful provisioning would be likely. The first time only two of the seven members favored making the attempt, and only one of the two, Secretary Chase, was confident that it could be made without armed conflict. The second time only one definitely opposed the attempt, but even Chase, who still favored it, had lost his confidence that it could be carried out peaceably. Secretary Welles, who had changed from opposition to approval, now expressed an opinion similar to Chase's. "There is little possibility that this will be permitted," Welles stated, "if the opposing forces can prevent it."

The objection may be raised that, nevertheless, Lincoln had reason to think *his* Sumter expedition, unlike Buchanan's, might be tolerated by the authorities in Charleston because he intended to give, and did give, advance notice of its coming, whereas Buchanan had not done so. Though Ramsdell has characterized this notice as a threat, and a double-barreled one at that, his critics have replied that it was no such thing. They say it was given "to show that hostile surprise was not intended" and to make clear Lincoln's "non-aggressive purpose." Whether the notification, with its reference to "men, arms, or ammunition," constituted a threat, we need not stop to debate. We need only to recall what Lincoln had learned recently from Hurlbut, his secret emissary to Charleston. Hurlbut reported his conclusion "that a ship known to contain *only provisions* for Sumpter would be stopped & refused admittance." In the light of this information, Lincoln would have had little ground for expecting that his notice would mollify the Confederates even if he had confined it to a simple announcement that he would attempt to supply "provisions only."

If Lincoln had intended and expected nothing but a peaceful provisioning, he no doubt would have been surprised and disappointed at the actual outcome. In fact, however, he repeatedly expressed a feeling of at least qualified satisfaction and success. When he replied to the Virginia delegates at the White House, on April 13, he said in an almost triumphant tone that the "unprovoked assault" would set him "at liberty" to go beyond the self-imposed limitations of his inaugural and to "repossess" as well as "hold, occupy, and possess" Federal positions in the seceded states. When he consoled the frustrated Fox, on May 1, he wrote: "You and I both anticipated that the cause of the country would be advanced by making the attempt to provision Fort Sumter, even if it should fail; and it is no small consolation now to feel that our anticipation is justified by the result." When he drafted his first message to Congress, for the July 4 session, he emphasized the point that, by the "affair at Fort Sumter," he had succeeded in making good his earlier declaration that, if war should come, the seceders would have to be the aggressors. And when he read the message to Browning, on July 3, he went on to remark, as Browning paraphrased him: "The plan succeeded. They attacked Sumter—it fell, and thus, did more service than it otherwise could."

In short, it appears that Lincoln, when he decided to send the Sumter expedition, considered hostilities to be *probable*. It also appears, however, that he believed an unopposed and peaceable provisioning to be at least barely *possible*. It is reasonable to suppose that he shared the expectation of his Attorney General, who wrote in his diary at the time Fox was leaving New York for Charleston: "One of two things will happen—either the fort will be well provisioned, the Southrons forebearing to assail the boats, or a fierce contest will ensue." If the first rather than the second of the two possibilities had materialized, then Lincoln doubtless could have said afterwards, just as he said when the second of the two occurred, that his plan had succeeded. Doubtless he would have been equally well satisfied, perhaps even better satisfied. Either way, whether the Confederates resisted or not, he would have been (in the words of Nicolay and Hay) "master of the situation."

It follows, then, that neither the Randall-Potter nor the Ramsdell view of Lincoln's intentions and expectations seems quite accurate. On the one hand, Lincoln did not count confidently upon peace, though he thought there was a bare chance of its being preserved for the time being. On the other hand, he did not deliberately provoke war. He thought hostilities would be the likely result, and he was determined that, if they should be, they must clearly be initiated by the Confederates. "To say that Lincoln meant that the first shot would be fired by the other side *if a first shot was fired*," as Randall has most admirably put the matter, "is not to say that he maneuvered to have the first shot fired."

The Ramsdell thesis, with its war-maneuver charge, is essentially an ꞌꞌort to document the rationalizations of Davis, Stephens, and other Confederates or Confederate sympathizers. Similarly, the Randall-Potter thesis, in one of its important aspects, is essentially an effort to substantiate the explanation that Lincoln gave after the events, in his July 4 message to Congress.

Interestingly, Potter observes that, to understand Lincoln's plans at the time of his inauguration, "it is necessary to exclude the misleading perspective of hindsight, and to view the problem as he viewed it at the time, rather than as he later viewed it." Yet, in dealing with Lincoln's policy after the inauguration, Potter neglects this very principle. Like Randall, he bases his argument largely on the misleading perspective of hindsight, on the way Lincoln viewed the problem in July rather than the way he viewed it in March and April.

According to Potter, who paraphrases Lincoln's July 4 message, the Sumter expedition was only tentative, the Pickens expedition definite. The Sumter expedition "was withheld until the fort was almost starved out, and it was withheld because Lincoln still hoped that he could transfer the issue of Union to Fort Pickens before the Sumter question reached a crisis." To both Potter and Randall the critical date is April 6. This was the date when, as Lincoln said in the message, he received a report that his order to land the troops already on shipboard in Pensacola Harbor, to reinforce Fort Pickens, had not been carried out. And this was the date when Lincoln sent to Major Anderson, by special messenger, the letter informing him that the expedition was going ahead (though the letter was dated April 4). "Up to April 6, then," Randall says, "the expedition, though prepared, could have been held back." And the plain implication of Randall and Potter,

as well as of Lincoln himself, is that if the troops had been landed at Fort Pickens, and if Lincoln had known of it by April 6, he would have called off the Sumter expedition.

There is undoubtedly an element of truth in this story of a Sumter-for-Pickens sacrifice. During March and early April the idea was discussed in the newspapers, was recommended by a number of Lincoln's Republican correspondents, and was urged again and again by Seward. At one time or another, Lincoln must have given some consideration to it. He could hardly have avoided doing so. Possibly, if he had been assured before March 29 that the troops had been landed and Fort Pickens was safe, he might not have decided at that time to prepare the Sumter expedition. But it appears (in the light of contemporary evidence) that, having ordered the Sumter preparations on March 29, he did not thereafter make his policy for Charleston contingent upon events at Pensacola.

Actually, the key dates regarding the Sumter decision are March 29 and April 4, not April 6. After the order for preparations had been given on March 29, there followed a period of vacillation and delay which was exasperating to Fox. The causes were twofold: the fears that visible preparations would hurt the prospects on the New York money market for the government loan to be subscribed on April 2, and the hopes (on the part of Seward) that a last-minute Sumter-for-Virginia deal could be arranged. After the successful sale of the bonds, and after the fiasco of Lincoln's conversation with the Virginia representative, Lincoln decided definitely to go ahead with the Sumter plans. On April 4 he arranged the details with Fox and wrote the letter informing Anderson that supplies would be on the way. That same day a copy of the letter was mailed to Anderson, and Anderson received it three days later. Not sure that the mail had got through, Lincoln sent the second copy by special messenger on April 6. His sending it on that day is no indication whatever that he waited until then to make his final decision regarding Sumter.

True, on April 6, Lincoln learned that his nearly-a-month-old order to land the troops at Pensacola had not been executed. But, to him, this was hardly unexpected news: it was merely a confirmation of what he already had guessed. As early as March 29 he had suspected that the order somehow had gone astray. On April 1 he was informed, by a communication from Pensacola, that the forces there had (as of March 21) been out of touch with the government. When the report of April 6 arrived, it had only one visible effect upon the administration: it caused the prompt dispatch of a messenger overland to Pensacola with new orders from Secretary Welles to land the troops already there.

Meanwhile, Seward had never given up his obsession with the idea of yielding Sumter and holding Pickens as a kind of substitute. The idea was Seward's, not Lincoln's. Seward stressed it in his brash April 1 memorandum, "Some Thoughts for the President's Consideration," and Lincoln in his written reply on the same day said his own domestic policy was the same as Seward's "with the single exception, that it does not propose to abandon Fort Sumter."

Why, then, did Lincoln tell Congress, in the July 4 message, that he *had* proposed to abandon Fort Sumter if Fort Pickens could be made secure in time? One conceivable reason is that, after the months of preoccupation with the widening war, he had forgotten some of the chronological details of his earlier policy

formation. He may well have remembered that on some occasion or other, possibly in mid-March, he had actually given at least fleeting consideration to the proposal. He may not have remembered exactly when, or how seriously. Another conceivable reason is that he was still concerned, in July, about the opinions of those peace-minded Northerners, including many Republicans, who in March and early April had been willing or even eager for Sumter to be evacuated on the condition that Pickens be firmly held. Lincoln may have felt it advisable now to reassure those timid and hesitant ones that he had, indeed, exhausted all the possibilities for peace and, in particular, had carefully considered the Sumter-for-Pickens alternative.

In stressing this alternative as an essential element of Lincoln's April policy, Randall and Potter confuse Lincoln's March and April thinking with Seward's. They make the same error in characterizing Lincoln's overall approach to the secession problem. Potter, for instance, asserts that "Republican policy was consistent" and that party leaders "insisted that delay and avoidance of friction would create a condition under which the Unionists in the South could regain the ascendancy." Certain party leaders, yes, and above all Seward, but Lincoln never fully shared Seward's faith in the do-nothing panacea.

In truth, Republican policy was far from being consistent. The policy of Seward was, at many points, inconsistent with that of Lincoln. The assumption that time would heal all wounds, the hints and promises of an early withdrawal from Sumter, the notion of bargaining Sumter for Virginia, the proposal to abandon Sumter and concentrate on Pickens—all these were hobbies of Seward's. Lincoln had great respect for Seward's abilities

and for his political value to the administration. He listened to Seward's sugges-
tions and urgings. To some extent he was
influenced by them, but he was by no
means converted. Nor did he authorize all
of Seward's undertakings. Some of them
he knew nothing about until after they
had been well advanced.

The worst fault in the Ramsdell thesis
is a lack of balance and perspective. Ramsdell makes Lincoln appear too much the
warmonger, Davis too much the peace
lover; Lincoln too much the controlling
force, Davis too much the passive agent.
Ramsdell argues that the Confederate
government "could not, without yielding
the principle of independence, abate its
claims to the fort." He fails to see that,
likewise, the Federal government could
not abate its claims without yielding the
principle of Union.

Davis made the decision that led directly to war. True, early on the morning
of April 12, Beauregard sent Roger A.
Pryor, James Chestnut, and two others
from Charleston to the fort to present
Davis's final terms, and these men on
their own rejected Anderson's reply—
which was that he would hold his fire and
evacuate in three days, unless he should
meanwhile receive "controlling instructions" or "additional supplies." Instead
of taking responsibility upon themselves,
Pryor and the other hot-headed under-
lings might have referred Anderson's
reply to Beauregard, and he in turn to
Walker and Davis. Since Pryor and his
colleagues went ahead without thus referring to higher authority, the story arose
that they and not Davis had made the real
decision. The story seemed to be confirmed by the testimony that Pryor gave
to an historian many years later, in 1909.
Accepting Pryor's account, the historian
wrote: "Pryor and his associates did not
report to the General, but, thinking that

Davis was trying to reconstruct the Union
and negotiate with Seward to that end and
that the chance of war was about to slip
away forever, they conferred together and
decided to give the signal to the gunners
to fire—and war began, and such a war!"
War began, all right, but the main point
of Pryor's testimony has no foundation in
fact. When Pryor and his associates rejected Anderson's reply, they were faith-
fully following the line of Davis's policy,
and Davis afterwards fully approved what
they had done. The real decision was his,
not theirs.

Davis justified his decision on the
ground that "the reduction of Fort Sumter
was a measure of defense rendered absolutely and immediately necessary." In
fact, however, Sumter in April, 1861,
offered no immediate threat to the physical safety of Charleston or of South Carolina or of the other six Confederate states.
Nor did the approach of Fox's small fleet
suddenly create such a threat. The landing of supplies—or even of men, arms,
and ammunition—would have made little
difference in the existing power balance.

Writers of the Ramsdell school insist
that there was no *military* reason for Lincoln's effort to provision the fort. They
cannot have it both ways. If there was no
military reason for Lincoln's attempt,
there could have been none for Davis' effort to forestall it.

Indeed, the Ramsdell thesis, turned inside out, could be applied to Davis with as
much justice as it has been applied to
Lincoln. One could argue that political
and not military necessity led Davis
to order the firing of the first shot.
The very life of the Confederacy, the
growth upon which that life depended,
was at stake. So were the pride, the prestige, and the position of Davis. Ramsdell
himself, a distinguished authority on
Confederate history, might appropriately
have devoted his talents to an essay on

"Davis and Fort Sumter" instead of "Lincoln and Fort Sumter."

Biographers of Davis and historians of the Confederacy have evaded or obscured their hero's role in the Sumter affair. They have digressed to levy accusations or innuendoes at Lincoln. If they have any concern for historical objectivity, however, they should face frankly the question of Davis's responsibility for the coming of the war. Upon them, upon *his* partisans, should rest the burden of proof. It should not have to be borne forever, as it has for far too many years, by Lincoln's champions. After all, Lincoln did not order the guns to fire. Davis did.

Authorities agree pretty well as to what actually happened in March and April, 1861. They disagree about the meaning of the events and, in particular, about the aims of Lincoln. To judge historical significance involves a certain amount of guessing, and to ascertain a man's intentions (especially when the man is so close-mouthed as Lincoln or, for that matter, Davis) requires a bit of mind reading. For these reasons, the true inwardness of the Sumter story will, in some of its aspects, always be more or less moot. The probable truth may be summarized as follows:

At the time of his inauguration Lincoln was determined to retake the Federal positions already lost to the seceding states as well as to hold the positions not yet lost. When he revised his inaugural, so as to announce only the "hold, occupy, and possess" objective, he did not really change or limit his original purpose. He meant to achieve this purpose, however, without appearing to initiate the use of force. He did not yet know precisely how he was going to manage so delicate a task, but he assumed that he would have plenty of time in which to deal with the problem.

Then, for about three weeks, he hesitated with regard to Fort Sumter, though not with regard to Fort Pickens, which he promptly ordered to be reinforced by means of the troops already available there. In the case of Sumter, the bad news from Anderson and the deterring counsel from Scott and the cabinet gave him pause. During the period of hesitation he considered alternative lines of action as at least temporary expedients—the collection of customs on ships off Southern ports, the evacuation of Sumter if and when Pickens had been made absolutely secure, the provisioning (with advance notice) but not the reinforcing of Sumter.

On March 29 he gave orders for the preparation of an expedition to provision Sumter—and also, conditionally, to reinforce it. He had decided to act because, from various sources of advice and information, he had concluded that a retreat at any point (except in the face of superior force) would lead eventually to a retreat at all points. If he were to yield to the demand for Sumter, he would still face the demand for Pickens and the other Florida forts, to say nothing of the demand for recognition of the Confederacy. True, if he took a stand, he would run the risk of antagonizing and losing Virginia and other still-loyal slave states. But if he declined to take a stand, he would still risk losing those states, through conferring new prestige and attractiveness upon the Confederacy. And, besides, he would surely alienate many of his adherents in the North.

Soon afterward, at Seward's urging, Lincoln ordered also the preparation of another expedition, this one to be secret, unannounced, and intended for the immediate reinforcement of Fort Pickens. Even its sponsor, Seward, did not expect the enterprise to be peaceably received: he merely thought Pensacola a better place than Charleston for war to begin. The Pickens expedition got off first, the Sumter preparations running into various snags, including Seward's efforts at sabotage.

On April 4, in consultation with Fox, Lincoln made the final arrangements for the Sumter effort. According to these carefully laid plans, Fox's men would try to run in supplies by boats or tugs. If challenged, the pilot would hand over a note explaining that the aim was only to take food to the garrison, and that if the Confederates fired upon the boats, they would be firing upon unarmed and defenseless men. Already the South Carolina governor would have received his notice. Thus the arrival of the boats would put the Confederates in a dilemma. If they fired, they would convict themselves of an atrocity. If not, they could hardly prevent the fort from being supplied. Either way, they would lose.

And if they fired, the guns of the warships offshore and of the fort itself would fire back and, hopefully, clear the way for the supplies to be taken in, along with reinforcements. This would, no doubt, entail a certain amount of bloodshed, but surely the Federal government would appear to be justified, in the eyes of most Northerners and of many Southerners as well. Even the majority of Virginians, under these circumstances, would possibly think twice before countenancing the secession of their state.

In certain respects the outcome was not to be quite what Lincoln anticipated.

The policy of the Montgomery government was less passive, less cautious, than he supposed. That policy aimed to get control of Sumter and the other forts as soon as it could be done, by negotiations if feasible, by siege or assault if not. The mission to Washington had a twofold function: on the one hand, to seek recognition of the Confederacy and a peaceful transfer of the forts and, on the other, to gain time for military preparations to be used in case diplomacy should fail. Once the preparations had proceeded far enough, the termination of diplomacy was to be the signal for the beginning of military measures. By early April, in Charleston, Beauregard was ready. Soon he would have begun actual operations for taking Sumter—even if Lincoln had never planned or sent an expedition of any kind (unless Anderson should promptly have given up, which was a possibility, or Lincoln should have invited the commissioners to talk with him, which was not).

When Davis heard of Lincoln's notice to the South Carolina governor, on April 8, his immediate response was to order Beauregard to prevent the landing of the supplies. It is interesting to speculate about what might have happened if Davis had stuck to this decision. Most likely, Beauregard then would have waited for the actual approach of the provisioning boats. But Fox, considering the storm-caused delays and the nonappearance of the flagship, *Powhatan*, probably would have decided not to send the boats in. In that event, the Sumter expedition would have proved an utter fiasco. Lincoln would have lost prestige and Davis gained it. Or, after hesitation, Fox might have made a token effort. Then things would have happened pretty much as Lincoln had calculated, except that the expedition would not have had the power to open the way for the supplies.

But Davis and his advisers did not remain content with their decision of April 8. Two days later they made a new one, and orders went to Beauregard to demand a surrender and, failing to get that, to reduce the fort.

This reaction, though more than Lincoln had counted on, was somewhat better, from his point of view, than the previous one. If the Confederates were going to fire at all, it was well that they should do so without even waiting until the food-laden boats were in sight. The eagerness of the Confederates would the more surely convict them of aggression, and this was all to the good, even though it would mean that Sumter would have less chance of being actually reinforced and held.

The first shot having been fired, the response of the North more than reconciled Lincoln to the loss of the fort, if not also to the loss of Virginia, Arkansas, Tennessee, and North Carolina. The response of the North certainly went far toward making possible the ultimate redemption of the Union.

In those early April days both Lincoln and Davis took chances which, in retrospect, seem awesome. The chances they took eventuated in the most terrible of all wars for the American people. Lincoln and Davis, as each made his irrevocable decision, could see clearly enough the cost of holding back. Neither could see so clearly the cost of going ahead. Both expected, or at least hoped, that the hostilities would be limited in space and time. Lincoln thought of blockade and boycott and a few seaborne operations against coastal forts. Davis thought of accessions and allies—in the slave states, in foreign countries, and in the North itself—which would make the Confederacy too strong for its independence to be long contested.

The Sumter incident itself did not lead at once to general war. Neither side was yet prepared for that. By a kind of escalation, however, war rapidly developed, and the lines were soon drawn. Through his proclamation of April 15, calling for 75,000 volunteers, Lincoln unintentionally contributed to the growth of the martial spirit on both sides. Perhaps if in that proclamation he had stressed his defensive purposes, especially the need for troops to protect the capital, he might at least have strengthened the Unionists in Virginia and the other non-seceded slave states.

The charge of "aggression," which has been bandied for so long, should not concern historians except as it figured in the propaganda of 1861 and after. From the Confederate point of view the United States had made itself the aggressor long before Lincoln acted to strengthen any fort. It was aggression when, on December 26, 1860, Major Anderson moved his small force from their exposed position at Fort Moultrie to the somewhat more secure one at Fort Sumter. Indeed, it was a continuing act of aggression every day that United States forces remained in Sumter or any other place within the boundaries of the Confederacy. And from the Union point of view the Confederacy had committed and was committing aggression by its very claim to existence, to say nothing of its seizures of Federal property and its preparations to seize Sumter and Pickens. Viewed impartially, both sides were guilty of aggression, and neither was.

When Lincoln expressed his desire for peace he was sincere, and so was Davis when he did the same. But Lincoln thought of peace for one, undivided country; Davis, of peace for two separate countries. "Both parties deprecated war," as Lincoln later put it, "but one of them would *make* war rather than let the nation survive; and the other would *accept* war rather than let it perish. And the war came."

Suggestions for Further Reading

The literature on the causes of the Civil War is so extensive that it has given rise to a number of convenient historiographical works, which may serve as a handy introduction to the subject. A full size well researched study of this type is Thomas J. Pressly, *Americans Interpret Their Civil War* (Princeton, 1954), which superseded the perceptive article by Howard K. Beale, "What Historians Have Thought About the Civil War," in *Theory and Practice in Historical Study*, Social Science Research Bulletin No. 54 (New York, 1946). Eric Foner's "The Causes of the Civil War: Recent Interpretations and New Directions," *Civil War History*, XX (1974), 197-214 brings the subject up to the date of publication. Edwin C. Rozwenc, ed., *The Causes of the Civil War* (Boston, 1972) is a useful collection of primary and secondary sources, as is Kenneth M. Stampp, ed., *The Causes of the Civil War* (Englewood Cliffs, N.J., 1974). Don E. Fehrenbacher, *Manifest Destiny and the Coming of the Civil War* (New York, 1970) and David Donald, *The Nation in Crisis* (New York, 1969) are two helpful bibliographies, as are the two volumes by Allan Nevins, James L. Robinson, Jr., and Bell I. Wiley, *Civil War Books: A Critical Bibliography* (2 vols., New York, 1967).

A series of one volume books covering the period may be helpful for the study of the causes of Civil War. The most comprehensive of these are J. G. Randall and David Donald, *The Civil War and Reconstruction* (2d ed., Boston, 1969), Peter Parish, *The American Civil War* (New York, 1975), and James M. McPherson, *Ordeal by Fire: The Civil War and Reconstruction* (New York, 1981). Other works include William H. Brock, *Conflict and Transformation: The United States, 1844-1877* (Baltimore, 1973), Robert Cruden, *The War That Never Ended: The American Civil War* (New York, 1977),

David Herbert Donald, *Liberty and Union: The Crisis of Popular Government, 1830-1860* (Boston, 1978), Donald M. Jacobs and Raymond H. Robinson, *America's Testing Time, 1844-1877* (Boston, 1973), Ludwell H. Johnson, *Division and Reunion: America 1848-1877* (Boston, 1973), Robert H. Jones, *Disrupted Decades: The Civil War and Reconstruction Years* (New York, 1973), David Lindsay, *Americans in Conflict: The Civil War and Reconstruction* (Boston, 1974), Thomas H. O'Connor, *The Disunited States: The Era of the Civil War and Reconstruction* (New York, 1978), David M. Potter, *Division and the Stresses of Reunion, 1846-1876* (New York, 1973), and Emory Thomas, *The American War and Peace, 1860-1877* (Englewood Cliffs, N.J., 1973).

Among the earlier works of participants and contemporaries, Horace Greeley, *The American Conflict* (2 vols., Hartford, 1864-1866), Henry Wilson, *History of the Rise and Fall of the Slave Power in America* (3 vols., Boston, 1872-1877), James G. Blaine, *Twenty Years of Congress* (2 vols., Norwich, Conn., 1884-1886), and John A. Logan, *The Great Conspiracy: Its Origin and History* (New York, 1886), are representative of the Northern point of view, generally emphasizing slavery (although Blaine well understood economic problems), and Edward A. Pollard, *The Lost Cause* (New York, 1866), Rushmore G. Horton, *A Youth's History of the Great Civil War in the United States, from 1861 to 1865 . . .* (New York, 1866), Jefferson Davis, *The Rise and Fall of the Confederate Government* (2 vols., New York, 1881), and Alexander H. Stephens, *A Constitutional View of the Late War Between the States* (2 vols., Chicago, 1868-1870), of the Southern, which either stressed abolitionism or constitutional issues.

In the half century following the Civil War,

the most important works written by historians generally nationalist in outlook are Hermann E. von Holst, *The Constitutional and Political History of the United States* (8 vols., Chicago, 1877-1892), James Schouler, *History of the United States under the Constitution* (7 vols., New York, 1880-1913), John W. Burgess, *The Middle Period 1817-1858* (New York, 1897) and *The Civil War and the Constitution* (2 vols., New York, 1901), and James Ford Rhodes, *History of the United States from the Compromise of 1850* (7 vols., New York, 1893-1906, and *Lectures on the Civil War* (New York, 1913). By and large, these writers deplored slavery and praised the superiority of a free society held together by a strong Union.

The best known example of the economic interpretation of the coming of the Civil War is Charles A. and Mary R. Beard, *The Rise of American Civilization* (2 vols., New York, 1927). Marxist variations of this theme include the earlier study by Algie Simons, *Social Forces in American History* (New York, 1911), Louis Hacker, *The Triumph of American Capitalism* (New York, 1940), and Philip S. Foner, *Business and Slavery* (Chapel Hill, N.C., 1941). A Marxist interpretation emphasizing the role of the Negro is Herbert Aptheker, *Essays in the History of the American Negro* (New York, 1945). More recent treatments include the appropriate chapters in William Appleman Williams, *The Contours of American History* (Cleveland, 1961), Barrington Moore, Jr., *Social Origins of Dictatorship and Democracy* (Boston, 1966), Eugene D. Genovese, *The World the Slaveholders Made* (New York, 1969), and Raimondo Luraghi, *La Storia della Guerra Civile Americana* (Turin, 1966).

The point of view stressing the existence of two different civilizations may be studied in Arthur C. Cole's *The Irrepressible Conflict, 1850-1865* (New York, 1934), Volume VII of Arthur M. Schlesinger and Dixon Ryan Fox, eds., *A History of American Life* (13 vols., New York, 1927-1948). Other books taking either this approach or focusing on the separate cultural developments of the sections include Edward Channing, *A History of the United States*, Vol. VI, *The War for Southern Independence* (New York, 1925), Jesse T. Carpenter, *The South as a Conscious Minority, 1789-*

1861 (New York, 1930), Ten Southerners, *I'll Take My Stand* (New York, 1930), especially the essay by Frank L. Owsley, *The Irrepressible Conflict,* stressing Southern loyalty to the agrarian ideal, Ulrich B. Phillips, "The Central Theme of Southern History," *The American Historical Review.* XXXIV (1928), 30-43, and his *The Course of the South to Secession* (New York, 1939), E.M. Coulter, ed., Rollin G. Osterweis, *Romanticism and Nationalism in the Old South* (New Haven, 1949), Clement Eaton, *The Growth of Southern Civilization, 1790-1860* (New York, 1961), and Eric Foner, *Free Soil, Free Labor, Free Men: The Ideology of the Republican Party before the Civil War* (New York, 1970). A variety of this approach is represented by Don E. Fehrenbacher, *The South and Three Sectional Crises* (Baton Rouge, 1980), which emphasizes the South's defense of its honor in the face of world-wide attacks on slavery as one of the causes of the war, and by William Barney, *The Road to Secession* (New York, 1972), which focuses on the expansive nature of Southern society as a disturbing factor.

The older revisionist school which stressed the failure of the political system was foreshadowed by the study of Mary Scrugham, *The Peaceable Americans of 1860-1861* (New York, 1921). It is best represented in the writings of James G. Randall. These include *The Civil War and Reconstruction* (Boston, 1937), since revised by David Donald from a different point of view (Boston, 1961, Lexington, 1969), and the best one volume study available, *Lincoln the Liberal Statesman* (New York, 1947), "The Blundering Generation," *The Mississippi Valley Historical Review,* XXVII (1940), 3-28, and his multivolume biography of Lincoln the President (see below). Avery O. Craven's *The Repressible Conflict, 1830-1861* (Baton Rouge, 1939), *The Coming of the Civil War* (New York, 1942), *The Growth of Southern Nationalism, 1848-1861* (Baton Rouge, 1953), and *Civil War in the Making, 1815-1860,* though later differing somewhat in approach, are examples of this school, which is also characterized by an anti-extremist position. George Fort Milton, *The Eve of the Conflict: Stephen A. Douglas and the Needless War* (New York, 1934), and Albert J. Beveridge, *Abraham Lincoln, 1809-1858* (2 vols., Boston, 1928), present the Senator from Illinois in a favorable light, while Philip G. Auchampaugh, *James Buchanan and His Cabinet on the Eve of Secession* (Lancaster, Pa., 1926) and Philip S. Klein, *President James Buchanan* (University Park, Pa., 1962) constitute attempts to rehabilitate the fifteenth President of the United States. Roy F. Nichols, *The Disruption of American Democracy* (New York, 1948) emphasizes the failure of the political system, especially the collapse of the Democratic party; David Donald, *An Excess of Democracy* (Oxford, 1960), stresses the institutional inability of the American people to meet the crisis, Michael F. Holt, *The Political Crisis of the 1850's* (New York, 1978), the breakdown of the second party system, and Arthur Bestor, "State Sovereignty and Slavery: A Reinterpretation of Pro-Slavery Constitutional Doctrine, 1846-1860," *Journal of the Illinois State Historical Society,* LIV (1961), 117-180, and "The American Civil War as a Constitutional Crisis," *The American Historical Review,* LXIX (1964), 327-352, focus once more on the constitutional issues which gave rise to the conflict.

The related problem of extremism is represented by such Southern oriented works as many of Craven's volumes, mentioned above, which put a great deal of blame on the abolitionists, Frank L. Owsley's "The Fundamental Cause of the Civil War: Egocentric Sectionalism," *Journal of Southern History,* VII (1941), 3-18, and Charles W. Ramsdell's "The Natural Limits of Slavery Expansion," *Mississippi Valley Historical Review,* XVI (1929), 151-171. Arnold Whitridge, *No Compromise: The Story of the Fanatics Who Paved the Way to the Civil War* (New York, 1960), takes a similar point of view, although the author is as critical of the fire-eaters as of the abolitionists. The other side is presented by Hans L. Trefousse, *The Radical Republicans: Lincoln's Vanguard for Racial Justice* (New York, 1969), and a more favorable treatment of abolitionist and radicals in general may be found in Dwight L. Dumond, *Anti-Slavery Origins of the Civil War in the United States* (Ann Arbor, 1939), Russell B. Nye, *Fettered Freedom* (Lansing, 1949), Louis Filler, *The Crusade Against Slavery* (New York, 1960),

James M. McPherson, *The Struggle for Equality: Abolitionists and Negroes in the Civil War and Reconstruction* (Princeton, 1964), James Brewer Stewart, *Holy Warriors: The Abolitionists and American Slavery* (New York, 1976), Richard H. Sewall, *Ballots for Freedom: Antislavery Politics in the United States, 1837-1860,* (New York, 1976) and Jane H. and William H. Pease, *Bound With Them in Chains: A Biographical History of the Antislavery Movement* (Westport, Conn., 1972). Gilbert Barnes, *The Antislavery Impulse* (New York, 1933), emphasizes the contributions of Western abolitionists, and Aileen S. Kraditor, *Means and Ends in American Abolitionism: Garrison and His Critics on Strategy and Tactics, 1834-1850* (New York, 1969), the importance of radicalism.

The most comprehensive post-World War II work, which stresses racial factors as well as slavery in spite of great fairness to the South, is Allan Nevins, *Ordeal of the Union* (2 vols., New York, 1947), *The Emergence of Lincoln* (2 vols., New York, 1950), and *The War for the Union* (4 vols., New York, 1959-1971). A similar explanation may be found in Kenneth P. Stampp, *The Imperiled Union* (New York, 1980). Bernard De Voto, in his remarks in "The Easy Chair," *Harper's Magazine,* CXCII (1946), 123-126, 234-237, severely criticizes the revisionists, as does Arthur Schlesinger, Jr., in "The Causes of the American Civil War: A Note on Historical Sentimentalism," *Partisan Review,* XIV (1949), 968-981, which seeks to reestablish the relevance of abolitionism and the earnestness of the antislavery crusade. This approach has been criticized by John S. Rosenberg in "Toward a New Civil War Revisionism," *American Scholar,* XXXVIII (Spring, 1969), 250-272, but the most important modern synthesis, David Potter's *The Impending Crisis, 1848-1861* (New York, 1976) once more attaches importance to the primacy of the slavery issue. Gerald Gunderson, "The Origins of the American Civil War," *Journal of Economic History,* XXXIV (1974), 915-950, in an economic treatment of the problem, comes to the same conclusion.

The entire institution of slavery has been subjected to a new and critical analysis, reversing, in many ways, the assessment in U. B. Phillips, *American Negro Slavery* (New York, 1918), and *Life and Labor in the Old South*

(Boston, 1929). Among these works are Kenneth M. Stampp, *The Peculiar Institution: Slavery in the Ante-Bellum South* (New York, 1956), Stanley M. Elkins, *Slavery: A Problem in American Institutional and Intellectual Life* (Chicago, 1949), John W. Blassingame, *The Slave Community* (New York, 1972), William Brion Davis, *The Problem of Slavery in Western Culture* (Ithaca, 1966), and *The Problem of Slavery in the Age of Revolution, 1770-1823* (Ithaca, 1975), Leslie Howard Owens, *This Species of Property: Slave Life and Culture in the Old South* (New York, 1976), Nathan Huggins, *Black Odyssey* (New York, 1977), and the Marxist interpretation by Eugene D. Genovese, *The Political Economy of Slavery* (New York, 1965), and *Roll, Jordan, Roll* (New York, 1974). Robert William Fogel and Stanley L. Engerman, *Time on the Cross: The Economics of American Negro Slavery* (Boston, 1974) is a highly controversial work ably refuted by Herbert G. Gutman, the author of *The Black Family in Slavery and Freedom, 1750-1925* (New York, 1976), in *Slavery and the Numbers Game* (Urbana, Ill., 1975).

The Southern view of the immediate causes of the Civil War is represented by Charles W. Ramsdell, "Lincoln and Fort Sumter," *Journal of Southern History,* III (1937), 259-288, and J. S. Tilley, *Lincoln Takes Command* (Chapel Hill, 1941). Sympathetic to Lincoln and the North are David M. Potter, *Lincoln and His Party in the Secession Crisis (2d ed., New Haven, 1962);* J. G. Randall, *Lincoln the President* (4 vols., New York, 1945-1955, final volume co-authored by Richard N. Current); W. A. Swanberg, *First Blood: The Story of Fort Sumter* (New York, 1958); Dwight I. Dumond, *The Secession Movement, 1860-1861* (New York, 1931); and, with modifications, Kenneth M. Stampp, *And the War Came: The North and the Secession Crisis* (Baton Rouge, 1950), and Richard N. Current, *Lincoln and the First Shot* (Philadelphia, 1963). Current's *The Lincoln Nobody Knows: Portrait in Contrasts of the Greatest American* (New York, 1958), contains an excellent chapter on the outbreak of the war. Whether or not the South was justified in seceding is the problem discussed by Arthur C. Cole, "Lincoln's Election an Immediate Menace to Slavery in the States?" *The American Historical Review,* XXXVI (1931), 740-767, who answers the question in the negative, and by J. G. de Roulhac Hamilton, "Lincoln's Election an Immediate Menace to Slavery in the States?" *The American Historical Review,* XXXVII (1932), 700-711, who comes to the opposite conclusion.

The problem of the irrepressible conflict has been reexamined by Pieter Geyl, "The American Civil War and the Problem of Inevitability," *New England Quarterly,* XXIV (1951), 147-168, and by Thomas A. Bonner, "Civil War Historians and the 'Needless War' Doctrine," *Journal of the History of Ideas,* XVII (1956), 193-216. Convenient collections of source material include Robert W. Johannsen, ed., *The Union in Crisis, 1850-1877* (New York, 1965), and Frank Moore, ed., *The Rebellion Record...* (12 vols., New York, 1862-1868).

free soilers → Pg 25→Jefferson
Davis's view on them